Potato Cookbook

100 Delicious Potato Recipes

By
BookSumo Press
All rights reserved

Published by
http://www.booksumo.com

ENJOY THE RECIPES?

KEEP ON COOKING WITH 6 MORE FREE COOKBOOKS!

Visit our website and simply enter your email address to join the club and receive your 6 cookbooks.

http://booksumo.com/magnet

https://www.instagram.com/booksumopress/

https://www.facebook.com/booksumo/

LEGAL NOTES

All Rights Reserved. No Part Of This Book May Be Reproduced Or Transmitted In Any Form Or By Any Means. Photocopying, Posting Online, And / Or Digital Copying Is Strictly Prohibited Unless Written Permission Is Granted By The Book's Publishing Company. Limited Use Of The Book's Text Is Permitted For Use In Reviews Written For The Public.

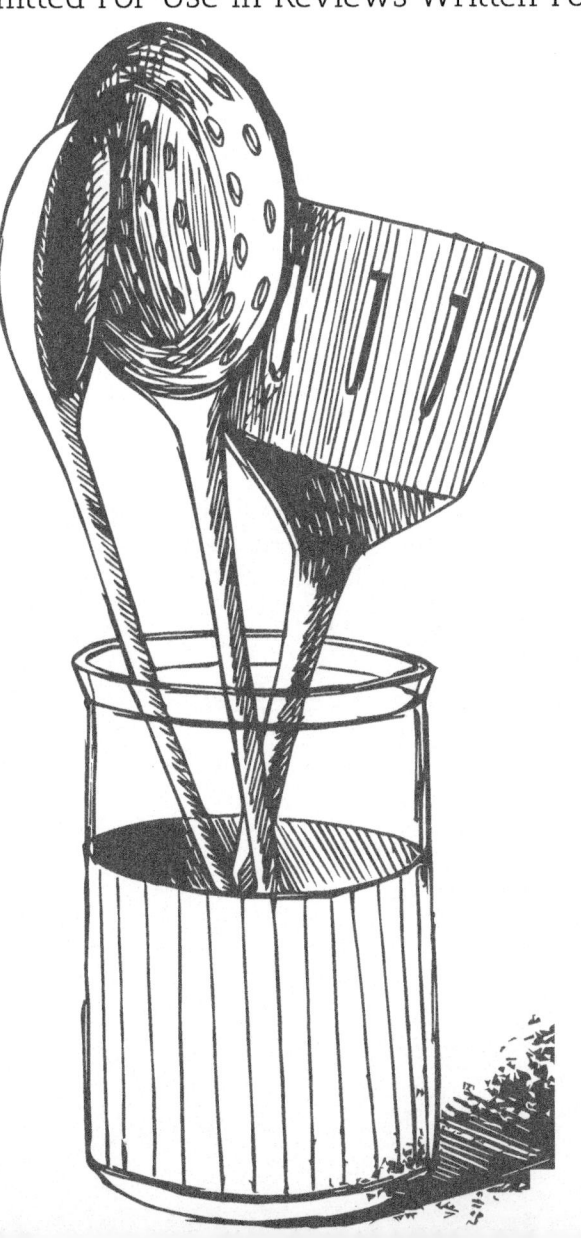

Table of Contents

Pears and Sweet Mashed Potatoes 9

Artisan Mashed Potatoes 10

Turkey Tarragon Mashed Potatoes 11

Mashed Potatoes for Autumn 12

Mashed Potatoes Indian Bread 13

Mashed Potatoes and Pesto 14

Mashed Potato Meatloaf 15

Beans and Mashed Potatoes 16

Mashed Potatoes and Gouda 17

Mashed Potatoes Cakes 18

Glazed Honey Veggies and Chicken Roast 19

Cottage Steak Soup 20

Chunky Corned Beef Soup 21

Bell Spanish Beef Soup 22

Crushed Idaho Soup 23

Classic Sirloin Soup 24

Hungarian Paprika Goulash Soup 25

Bell Green Beef Soup 26

Meaty Potato Surprise 27

Santa Ana Pie 28

Vidalia Potato and Noodles Pierogi Bake 29

Pecan and Sweet Potato Casserole 30

Potatoes and Kielbasa 31

Italian Style Beef & Veggies Pierogies Skillet 32

Wonton Cheddar Pierogies 33

Double Stuffed Pierogies 34

The Brooklyn Style Sandwich 35

Latkes 36

Cranberries and Potatoes 37

Sun Skillet 38

Baked Greek Potatoes 39

Minty Potato Salad 40

Saucy Greens Potato Salad 41

Algerian Poached Eggs 42

Sweet Potato Casserole 43

Potatoes and Garlic 44

Sweet Potatoes II 45

Baked Potatoes Remix 46

Dip for Baked Potatoes 47

Mushroom and Onion Baked Potato 48

Wedges Done Right 49

Classic Cracked Potato & Beef Roast 50

Italian Countryside Fries 51

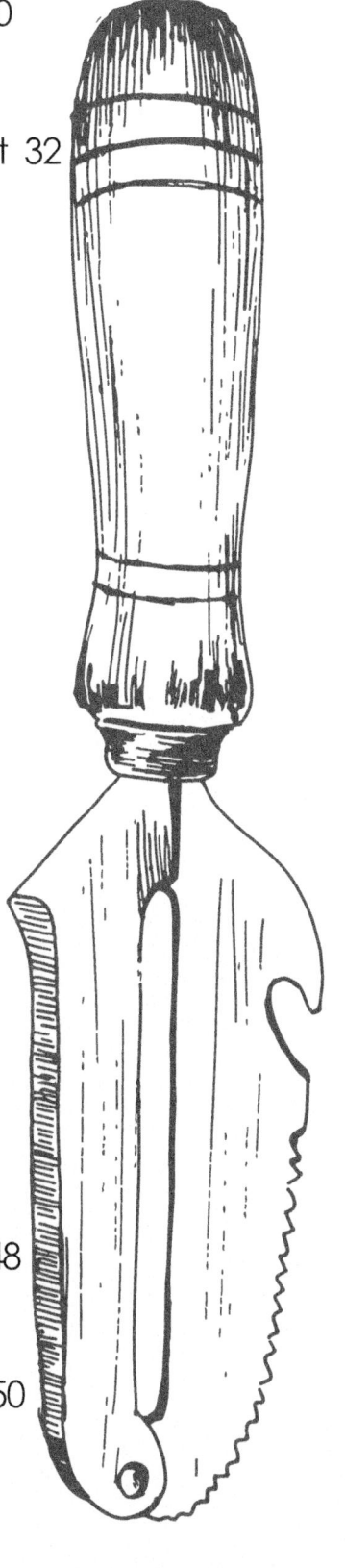

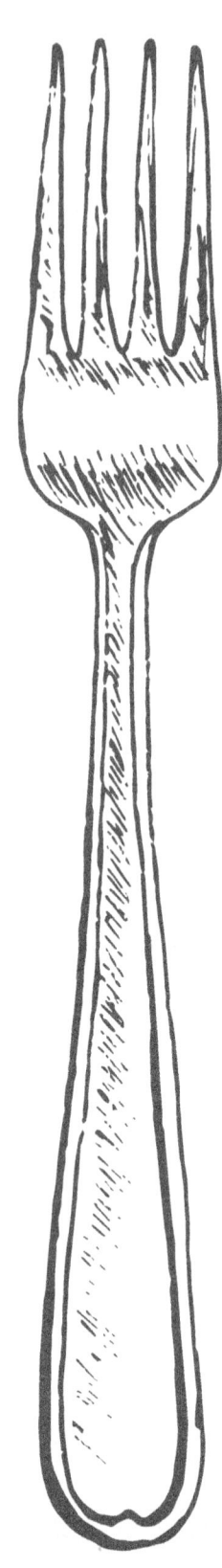

Hot Pepper White Pepper French Fries 52

English Salt & Vinegar Fries 53

3-Ingredient French Fries 54

4-Ingredient Classicals 55

Parmesan Onions and Fries 56

Cajun Spice Mix 57

How to Bake French Fries 58

Louisiana Creole Fries 59

Copycat Fast Food Franchise Fries 60

Russet Roast Stew 61

Onion Soup Roast 62

Potato Roast 63

Roasted Italian Cheesy Veggies 64

Smoked Feta Frittata 65

Cabbage from Russia 66

Maggie's Easy Cauliflower Soup 67

Saucy Cabbage Beef Soup 68

Golden Chuck Roast Soup 69

Italian Chunky Mushroom Soup 70

Chile Sauerkraut Soup 71

Green Pepper Sunday Hash 72

Tropical Mango Stew 73

Everything Curry Dinner 74

Peanut Butter Coconut Curry 75

Jamaican Curry Chicken I 76

The Canadian Frittata 77

Tomato and Potato Frittata 78

The Classical Morning Frittata 79

Cheesy Beef & Potato Casserole 80

Veggie Scrambled Eggs 81

Herbed Sweet Potato Frittata 82

Balsamic Roasted Veggies 83

Zesty Veggies Roast 84

Cherry Potato Roast Salad 85

Vegetarian Curry Japanese Style 86

Dublin Dumplings 88

Turkey Stew with Buttermilk Dumplings 89

Baked Golden Chicken and Potato 90

Authentic New England Style Clam Chowder 91

Potatoes, Corn, and Steak Soup 92

Turkey Leg Soup 93

Pierogi Milanese 94

6-Ingredient Pierogies 95

White Tuna Pierogi Bake 96

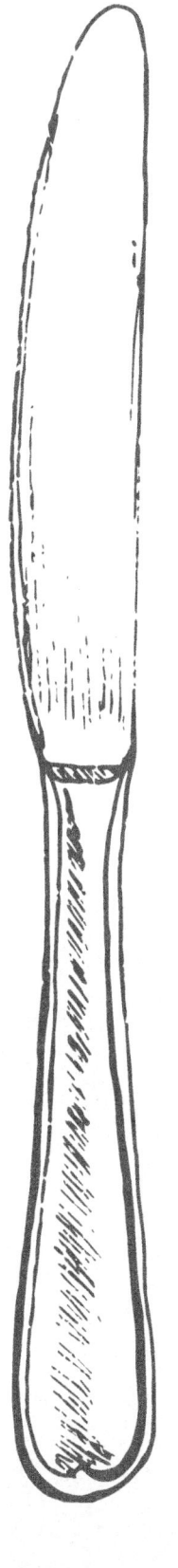

Pierogi Tortilla 97

Sweet and Salty Dumplings 98

Sharp Cheesy Potato Casserole 99

A Vegan's Potato Soup 100

Beef Based Corn Potato Soup 101

Vegetable Soup from Bogota 102

Pears and Sweet Mashed Potatoes

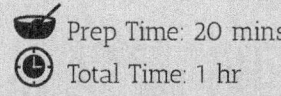

Prep Time: 20 mins
Total Time: 1 hr

Servings per Recipe: 8
Calories	257 kcal
Fat	7.8 g
Carbohydrates	44.6g
Protein	2.8 g
Cholesterol	20 mg
Sodium	201 mg

Ingredients

3 lbs sweet potatoes, cleaned, dried
1/3 C. butter
1 (15.25 oz.) can pears in syrup
2 tbsps chopped fresh sage

Salt and black pepper

Directions

1. Set your oven to 425 degrees before doing anything else.
2. Pierce your sweet potatoes with a toothpick and cook them in the oven for 55 mins.
3. At the same time heat and stir your butter for 11 mins then shut the heat.
4. Cut your potatoes into halves and remove the insides into the pot with butter.
5. Mash the potatoes with the sage and pears in the butter and get everything hot.
6. Add some pepper and salt.
7. Enjoy.

ARTISAN
Mashed Potatoes

🥣 Prep Time: 15 mins
🕒 Total Time: 35 mins

Servings per Recipe: 4
Calories   320 kcal
Fat   17.8 g
Carbohydrates   37.6 g
Protein   5.6 g
Cholesterol   51 mg
Sodium   333 mg

Ingredients

2 russet potatoes, peeled and cut into chunks
1 large celery root, peeled and cut into chunks
1/4 C. butter
1 pinch freshly grated nutmeg, or to taste
salt and freshly ground black pepper to taste
1/4 C. heavy whipping cream

Directions

1. Get your celery and potatoes boiling in water and salt for 25 mins then remove the liquids and combine everything together.
2. Get a bowl and begin to mash the potatoes with some black pepper, butter, salt, and nutmeg.
3. Then add in the cream and mash everything again.
4. Enjoy.

Turkey Tarragon Mashed Potatoes

Prep Time: 15 mins
Total Time: 30 mins

Servings per Recipe: 10
Calories	240 kcal
Fat	3.2 g
Carbohydrates	42.9 g
Protein	11 g
Cholesterol	13 mg
Sodium	372 mg

Ingredients

- 1 (12 oz.) package turkey bacon
- 5 lbs russet potatoes, peeled and diced
- 1 (32 oz.) carton chicken Stock
- 1/4 C. low-fat sour cream
- 1/4 C. low-sodium dry ranch dressing mix
- 3/4 C. shredded nonfat Cheddar cheese
- 1 tbsp chopped fresh chives
- 2 tbsps tarragon

Directions

1. Fry your bacon until fully done then break it into pieces as you remove it from the pan.
2. Get your potatoes boiling in broth for 17 mins then shut the heat.
3. Add in the ranch and sour cream.
4. Mash the potatoes until they are smooth and creamy with a mixer for 5 mins then add in the chives, tarragon, cheddar, and bacon.
5. Stir everything again.
6. Enjoy.

MASHED POTATOES
for Autumn

Prep Time: 20 mins
Total Time: 35 mins

Servings per Recipe: 8	
Calories	213 kcal
Fat	6.5 g
Carbohydrates	35.7 g
Protein	4.3 g
Cholesterol	17 mg
Sodium	519 mg

Ingredients

2 lbs russet potatoes, peeled and cut into cubes
1 lb sweet potatoes, peeled and cut into cubes
1 tbsp chicken bouillon granules
3/4 C. milk, warmed
1/4 C. butter

1 1/2 tbsps brown sugar
1 tsp salt
1/4 tsp ground white pepper
1/4 tsp allspice
1/8 tsp ground nutmeg

Directions

1. Get both types of potatoes boiling in water with the bouillon.
2. Once the potatoes are boiling, set the heat to medium and continue to cook them for 22 mins.
3. Now remove all the liquids and mash the potatoes partially.
4. Add in: the nutmeg, milk, allspice, butter, pepper, brown sugar, and salt.
5. Begin to mash the potatoes again until everything is smooth.
6. Enjoy.

Mashed Potatoes Indian Bread

Prep Time: 30 mins
Total Time: 45 mins

Servings per Recipe: 4
Calories   400 kcal
Fat   18.6 g
Carbohydrates   53.1g
Protein   9.3 g
Cholesterol   9 mg
Sodium   183 mg

Ingredients

1 C. mashed potatoes
salt to taste
1/2 tsp cayenne pepper
1/2 tsp ground turmeric
1 tbsp fresh cilantro, finely chopped
3 tbsps vegetable oil

2 C. whole wheat flour
3/4 C. vegetable oil for frying
1 tbsp butter, melted

Directions

1. Get a bowl, combine: 3 tbsps veggie oil, mashed potatoes, cilantro, salt, turmeric, cayenne, and salt.
2. Now slowly add in the wheat flour then work the mix into a dough.
3. Place the dough in bowl coated with oil and place a covering of plastic on the bowl.
4. Let the dough sit for 12 mins.
5. Now begin to heat a griddle coated with nonstick spray.
6. Break your dough into balls then flatten the balls to a quarter of an inch.
7. Fry the flattened dough in 1 tsp of oil for each side.
8. Keep frying the bread until brown portions begin to show.
9. Top each piece with some butter.
10. Enjoy.

MASHED POTATOES
and Pesto

Prep Time: 5 mins
Total Time: 30 mins

Servings per Recipe: 4
Calories 216 kcal
Fat 5.1 g
Carbohydrates 38.2g
Protein 5.5 g
Cholesterol 10 mg
Sodium 69 mg

Ingredients

4 medium potatoes, peeled and cubed
1 tbsp butter
1/4 C. milk, or as needed

1 tbsp basil pesto

Directions

1. Get your potatoes boiling in water for 15 mins then remove all the liquids.
2. Begin to the mash the potatoes partially then add in the milk and butter.
3. Continue to mash the potatoes then add in the pesto and keep mashing everything until the pesto is evenly distributed and the potatoes are smooth.
4. Enjoy.

Mashed Potato Meatloaf

Prep Time: 15 mins
Total Time: 1 hr 15 mins

Servings per Recipe: 6
Calories	396 kcal
Fat	23.8 g
Carbohydrates	16 g
Protein	27.8 g
Cholesterol	122 mg
Sodium	979 mg

Ingredients

- 1 C. diced onion
- 1 C. instant mashed potatoes
- 1 C. diced green bell pepper
- 1/4 C. hot pepper sauce
- 1 egg
- 1 tsp salt
- 1 tsp ground black pepper
- 2 lbs ground beef
- 1 (.75 oz.) packet dry brown gravy mix

Directions

1. Set your oven to 350 degrees before doing anything else.
2. Get a bowl, combine: pepper, onion, salt, bell pepper, eggs, instant potatoes, and hot sauce.
3. Stir the mix then add in the beef and combine everything evenly.
4. Place the beef into a bread pan and top it with the gravy mix.
5. Cook the meatloaf in the oven for 60 mins then let it sit for 15 mins before slicing it into pieces.
6. Enjoy.

BEANS
and Mashed Potatoes

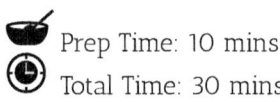

Prep Time: 10 mins
Total Time: 30 mins

Servings per Recipe: 8
Calories	119 kcal
Fat	7.4 g
Carbohydrates	10.5g
Protein	2.1 g
Cholesterol	2 mg
Sodium	507 mg

Ingredients

1 (4 oz.) package Idahoan(R) Buttery Homestyle Flavored Mashed Potatoes, prepared
1 (10.75 oz.) can condensed cream of mushroom soup
3/4 C. milk
1/8 tsp ground black pepper

2 (15 oz.) cans green beans, drained*
1 1/3 C. French's(R) French Fried Onions, divided

Directions

1. Set your oven to 350 degrees before doing anything else.
2. Get a bowl, combine: green beans, soup, pepper, and milk.
3. Stir the mix then add in 2/3 C. of fried onions.
4. Spread everything into a baking dish and top the dish with some of the potatoes.
5. For 4 mins toast everything under the broiler then add the rest of the fried onions.
6. Enjoy.

Mashed Potatoes and Gouda

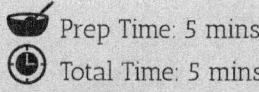 Prep Time: 5 mins
Total Time: 5 mins

Servings per Recipe: 4
Calories   128 kcal
Fat   8.6 g
Carbohydrates   0.3g
Protein   12.7 g
Cholesterol   32 mg
Sodium   783 mg

Ingredients

- 1 (4 oz.) package Idahoan(R) Buttery Golden Selects Mashed Potatoes
- 1 (3 oz.) package bacon bits*
- 1/2 C. Gouda cheese, shredded

Directions

1. Cook your potatoes in line with its associated directions then add in the cheese and bacon.
2. Stir the bacon and cheese into the potatoes.
3. Enjoy.

MASHED POTATOES
Cakes

Prep Time: 15 mins
Total Time: 25 mins

Servings per Recipe: 6
Calories	261 kcal
Fat	12.8 g
Carbohydrates	29.2g
Protein	7.2 g
Cholesterol	43 mg
Sodium	335 mg

Ingredients

- 1 1/2 C. grated raw potatoes
- 1 C. all-purpose flour
- 1/2 C. shredded Cheddar cheese
- 1 C. leftover mashed potatoes
- 1/4 tsp salt
- 1/4 tsp ground black pepper
- 1 egg
- 2 tbsps ranch dressing
- 1 tbsp milk
- 2 tbsps vegetable oil

Directions

1. Get a bowl, combine: the flour and potatoes.
2. Add in the cheese, some pepper, and salt.
3. Stir the cheese into the potatoes.
4. Get a 2nd bowl, combine: milk, egg, and ranch dressing.
5. Once the mix is smooth combine both bowls and stir everything again.
6. Now get your veggie oil hot for frying then fry tbsp sized dollops of the mix in the pan for 5 mins each side.
7. Enjoy.

Glazed Honey Veggies and Chicken Roast

🥣 Prep Time: 20 mins
🕐 Total Time: 1 hr 10 mins

Servings per Recipe: 4
Calories   557.6
Fat   28.4 g
Cholesterol   103.5 mg
Sodium   298.1 mg
Carbohydrates   45.9 g
Protein   31.2 g

Ingredients

- 1 lb potato, scrubbed and cut into wedges
- 2 lbs chicken
- 6 medium carrots, scrubbed and sliced
- 2 tbsp olive oil
- 1 1/2 tbsp honey
- 3 tbsp mustard
- 1 tsp rosemary
- 2 heads garlic
- salt and pepper

Directions

1. Before you do anything set the oven to 425 F.
2. Get a large bowl: Stir in it the carrots with onion, oil, some salt and pepper. Spread the mix on a roasting dish and top them with the garlic
3. Place the rosemary on top followed by the chicken. Cook them in the oven for 32 min.
4. Get a small bowl: Mix in it the mustard with honey. Transfer the chicken to a plate and smother it with the honey mix.
5. Mix the veggies and place the chicken back in the pan. Cook the roast for 18 min then serve it warm.
6. Enjoy.

COTTAGE
Steak Soup

Prep Time: 20 mins
Total Time: 8 hrs 20 mins

Servings per Recipe: 6
Calories   127.2
Fat   0.9 g
Cholesterol   0.3 mg
Sodium   990.8 mg
Carbohydrates   25.1 g
Protein   5.9 g

Ingredients

1 lb boneless round steak, cubed
1 (14 oz.) can diced tomatoes, do not drain
24 fluid oz. beef broth
3 beef bouillon cubes
2 medium potatoes, peeled and cubed
2 medium onions, chopped
2 celery ribs, sliced
2 carrots, chopped

1/2 tsp basil
1/2 tsp oregano
1/2 tsp thyme
1 bay leaf
1/4 tsp pepper
1 C. fresh peas or 1 C. frozen peas

Directions

1. Stir all the ingredients in a slow cooker. Put on the lid and the soup for 7 h 30 min on low.
2. Adjust the seasoning of the soup then serve it warm.
3. Enjoy.

Chunky Corned Beef Soup

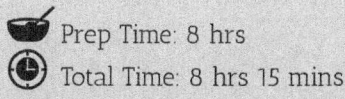

Prep Time: 8 hrs
Total Time: 8 hrs 15 mins

Servings per Recipe: 12
Calories   142.4
Fat   1.2 g
Cholesterol   0.2 mg
Sodium   737.6 mg
Carbohydrates   31.5 g
Protein   4.7 g

Ingredients

- 2 lbs stew beef chunks
- 15 oz. crushed tomatoes
- 1 lb baby carrots
- 2 stalks celery, with tops Sliced
- 2 onions, Diced
- 4 red potatoes, Diced
- 3 C. water
- 1 tsp salt
- 1 tsp black pepper
- 4 beef bouillon cubes
- 15 oz. corn
- 2 C. fresh green beans, snapped and cut into 1 inch pieces (frozen is ok)
- 10 oz. tomato soup
- 10 oz. water (soup can)
- 1 bay leaf
- 1 tbsp Worcestershire sauce

Directions

1. Stir all the ingredients in a slow cooker. Put on the lid and the soup for 7 h 30 min on low.
2. Adjust the seasoning of the soup then serve it warm.
3. Enjoy.

BELL
Spanish Beef Soup

🍲 Prep Time: 25 mins
⏱ Total Time: 1 hr 40 mins

Servings per Recipe: 6
Calories 973.9
Fat 3.2 g
Cholesterol 0 mg
Sodium 91.1 mg
Carbohydrates 215.2 g
Protein 22.4 g

Ingredients

5 lbs stew beef bones
Salt, to taste
Garlic powder, to taste
4 ears corn, husked an cut in half
6 celery ribs, cut into 1/2-inch pieces
3 carrots, peeled and cut into 1-inch pieces
4 potatoes, peeled and cut into 2-inch chunks
3 tomatoes cut into wedges
3 zucchini, cut into 2-inch chunks
2 onions cut into 6 wedges
1/2 head cabbage, cut into quarters
1 green bell pepper, sliced
6 C. rice, Spanish rice, cooked and hot
1 lemon, cut into 6 wedges

Directions

1. Place a large soup pot over medium heat. Place the beef bones it and cover 6 inches of the pot with water.
2. Them until they start boiling. Lower the heat and simmer them for 50 min.
3. Add the salt, garlic powder. Then add corn, celery and carrots. Bring them to a rolling boil for 17 min.
4. Stir in the potatoes, tomatoes, zucchini, onion, cabbage, and bell pepper. Bring them to a rolling boil for 17 min.
5. Serve your soup hot with the Spanish rice and lemon wedges.
6. Enjoy.

Crushed Idaho Soup

Prep Time: 25 mins
Total Time: 35 mins

Servings per Recipe: 6
Calories   335.9
Fat   10.4 g
Cholesterol   61.4 mg
Sodium   378.9 mg
Carbohydrates   37.5 g
Protein   24.9 g

Ingredients

- 1 1/4 lbs lean ground beef
- 1 (28 oz.) can crushed tomatoes
- 2 1/2 C. water
- 1/2 C. barley
- 3 large carrots (about 8 oz..
- 2 stalks celery
- 1 large Idaho potato (about 10 oz.)
- 1 medium onion (about 6 oz.)
- 1 clove garlic
- 1/2 tsp dried basil
- 1/2 tsp dried thyme leaves
- 1/2 tsp dried rosemary
- 1/2 tsp dried marjoram
- 1/4 tsp salt
- Fresh ground black pepper

Directions

1. Get a pressure cooker: press the sauté button on it and heat it. Add the beef and it for 10 min. discard the fat.
2. Stir in the tomatoes, water and barley. Put on the lid and bring the pot to pressure. The soup for 10 min on high pressure
3. Dice the onion and potato. Mince the garlic. Cut the carrots into thick sticks.
4. Use the natural method to release the pressure. Add the rest of the ingredients. Put on the lid and bring the pot to pressure. The soup for 10 min on high pressure
5. Use the natural method to release the pressure.
6. Adjust the seasoning of the soup then serve it warm.
7. Enjoy.

CLASSIC
Sirloin Soup

🥣 Prep Time: 30 mins
🕐 Total Time: 2 hrs 30 mins

Servings per Recipe: 6
Calories 406.6
Fat 7.3 g
Cholesterol 26.1 mg
Sodium 1232.5 mg
Carbohydrates 71.3 g
Protein 17.8 g

Ingredients

1/2 lb ground sirloin or 1/2 lb sliced roast beef, leftover
6 C. beef broth
1/2 C. fresh parsley, chopped
7 whole garlic cloves
2 C. carrots, peeled and in chunks
2 C. stewed tomatoes
1/2 C. green beans, sliced
1/2 C. broth
1 tsp salt
2 1/2 C. yellow onions, coarsely chopped
8 potatoes, peeled and cubed
1 C. celery, diced
1/2 C. corn
1/4 tsp garlic powder
Basil
Oregano, to taste

Directions

1. Season the sirloin with 1/4 tsp of garlic powder, some salt and pepper.
2. Place a large soup pot over medium heat. Add the beef and it for 6 min. Stir in the rest of ingredients.
3. Put on the lid and the soup for 1 h 35 min. Adjust the seasoning of the soup then serve it warm.
4. Enjoy.

Hungarian Paprika Goulash Soup

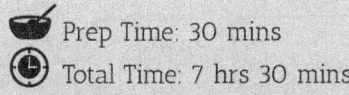

Prep Time: 30 mins
Total Time: 7 hrs 30 mins

Servings per Recipe: 5
Calories   387.4
Fat   14.4 g
Cholesterol   66.2 mg
Sodium   642.4 mg
Carbohydrates   40.2 g
Protein   25.7 g

Ingredients

- 1 tbsp vegetable oil
- 1 lb boneless bottom round steak cut in 1-inch cubes
- 1/4 tsp salt (to taste)
- 1/4 tsp black pepper
- 1 large onion, chopped
- 1 red bell pepper, chopped
- 1/4 C. all-purpose flour
- 2 garlic cloves, minced
- 3 tbsp sweet Hungarian paprika
- 1 tsp caraway seed
- 4 -5 small potatoes, cut in 1/2-inch rounds
- 2 1/2 C. beef broth (extra strength)
- 1 C. water
- 1 C. tomato puree
- Sour cream (for garnish)

Directions

1. Place a large skillet over medium heat. Add the oil and heat it. In it the beef in batches for 4 min per batch Drain the beef dices and place them aside. Season them with some salt and pepper.
2. Add a splash of oil to the skillet and heat it. Stir in the bell pepper with onion and them for 6 min. Stir in the flour, garlic, paprika, and caraway. Them for 1 min
3. Lay the potato slices in the bottom of a greased slow cooker. Top it with the veggies and beef followed by the broth, water and tomato puree.
4. Put on the lid. The soup for 7 h on low Adjust the seasoning of the soup then serve it warm.
5. Enjoy.

BELL
Green Beef Soup

🥣 Prep Time: 20 mins
🕐 Total Time: 5 hrs 20 mins

Servings per Recipe: 6
Calories   186.7
Fat   4.6 g
Cholesterol   17.5 mg
Sodium   1012.7 mg
Carbohydrates   29.6 g
Protein   9 g

Ingredients

1/3 lb ground beef
1/2 C. onion, chopped
1/4 C. celery, chopped
1/4 C. green pepper, chopped
2 garlic cloves, pressed
2 carrots, sliced
2 medium potatoes, cubed
1 zucchini, sliced & quartered
1 C. green beans, pieces
1 (28 oz.) can crushed tomatoes
2 bay leaves

1 tsp basil
1 tsp oregano
1 tsp thyme
2 tsp parsley
1/2 tbsp sugar
1 tbsp Worcestershire sauce
4 beef bouillon cubes
2 chicken bouillon cubes
3 C. water

Directions

1. Place a large crockpot over medium heat. Add the beef with onion, celery, green pepper, and garlic. Them for 8 min
2. Pour the water in a large saucepan and it until it starts boiling. Add the beef & chicken bouillon then stir them well. Transfer the mix to the soup pot.
3. Put on the lid and the soup for 2 h 30 min on high or 5 h on low.
4. Adjust the seasoning of the soup then serve it warm.
5. Enjoy.

Meaty Potato Surprise

Prep Time: 1 hr
Total Time: 1 hr 30 mins

Servings per Recipe: 4
Calories   791
Fat   38.9 g
Cholesterol   192.5 mg
Sodium   284.6 mg
Carbohydrates   47.6 g
Protein   55.1 g

Ingredients

4 medium russet potatoes (peeled, sliced and cooked)
2 lbs lean ground beef
4 tbsps butter, divided
1 large onion, chopped
1 tbsp garlic (or to taste)
1 red bell pepper, seeded and chopped
1 green bell pepper, seeded and chopped
1/4 C. grated parmesan cheese (optional)
salt and pepper

2 - 4 tbsps broth
1/4 C. chopped fresh parsley
1/4 C. milk
1/2 C. Swiss cheese, shredded

Directions

1. Before you do anything, heat the oven to 350 degrees F. Grease a 2-1/2 quart casserole dish.
2. In a heavy frying pan, the beef in 2 tbsp. butter until evenly browned. Stir in onion, both types of bell peppers, and garlic. Sauté until soft and then drain the excess fat.
3. Add salt, black pepper, sherry, parsley, and parmesan cheese. Sauté for no more than 7 minutes.
4. Pour the mixture into the baking dish.
5. Add the rest of the butter and milk to the cooked potatoes, and beat them until smooth. Add salt and black pepper if you want.
6. Spread the potatoes over the meat, covering all corners. Use a spoon to push the potato mixture tightly around the corners and side.
7. Cover the top with cheddar cheese (or parmesan cheese). Place the dish uncovered into the oven and book for 27-32 minutes, or until the potatoes and cheese turns light brown.
8. Enjoy.

SANTA ANA Pie

Prep Time: 10 mins
Total Time: 2 hrs 10 mins

Servings per Recipe: 4
Calories   1886.7
Fat   189.7 g
Cholesterol   255.7 mg
Sodium   698.4 mg
Carbohydrates   14 g
Protein   25.9 g

Ingredients

- 2 tbsps olive oil
- 6 slices turkey bacon, coarsely chopped
- 1 onion, finely sliced
- 2 garlic cloves, finely chopped
- 1/2 C. broth
- 1 kg beef, topside trimmed of fat, cut into 3cm pieces
- 1 1/2 C. tomato puree
- 1 C. reduced-beef broth
- 2 tbsps Kikkoman naturally brewed soy sauce
- 2 bay leaves
- 200 g large flat mushrooms
- chopped parsley, and
- mashed potatoes, to serve

Directions

1. Before you do anything, heat the oven to 350 degrees F.
2. Pour half of the oil into a flameproof baking dish. Place the dish over medium high heat.
3. Add 1/3 of the beef. Cook until it is brown on all sides, then set aside. Repeat this step two more times, setting aside the well-browned meat every time.
4. Lower heat to medium and add the rest of the oil. Stir in the onion, garlic, and bacon. Cook until the onion becomes tender.
5. Add broth and stir the contents of the dish well, dislodging any Ingredients that got stuck to the bottom of the dish.
6. Add the beef, stock, soy sauce, tomato puree, bay leaves, and mushrooms. Cover the dish and bake in the oven for 90 minutes, or until the beef becomes tender.
7. Uncover the dish and for another 17 minutes, or until there is little liquid.
8. Take the dish out of the oven and let it stand for 10 minutes. Top the pie with parsley and serve it from the dish.
9. Serve mashed potatoes separately.
10. Enjoy.

Vidalia Potato and Noodles Pierogi Bake

Prep Time: 10 mins
Total Time: 30 mins

Servings per Recipe: 4
Calories 579.0
Fat 28.8g
Cholesterol 122.8mg
Sodium 764.2mg
Carbohydrates 58.5g
Protein 21.7g

Ingredients

1/2 lb wide egg noodles, cooked
1/4 C. butter
1 1/2 C. mashed potatoes, prepared
5 slices American cheese
1/2 C. cheddar cheese, shredded
1/2 C. mozzarella cheese, shredded
1/4 large Vidalia onion, minced
2 garlic cloves, minced
salt and pepper, to taste

Directions

1. Before you do anything, preheat the oven to 350 F. Grease a casserole dish with a cooking spray.
2. Prepare the noodles by following the instructions on the package.
3. Place a large pan over medium heat: Heat in it the butter. Cook in it the garlic with onion, a pinch of salt and pepper.
4. Cook them for 5 min. Spread half of the lasagna sheets in the greased dish.
5. Spread over it half of the cheese followed by all the potato. Season them with some salt and pepper.
6. Cover it with the remaining pasta and cheese. Dot it with butter then bake it for 12 min.
7. Allow the lasagna casserole to rest for 5 min then serve it.
8. Enjoy.

PECAN and Sweet Potato Casserole

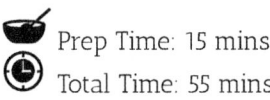

Prep Time: 15 mins
Total Time: 55 mins

Servings per Recipe: 6
Calories   570 kcal
Fat   40.8 g
Carbohydrates   47.9 g
Protein   6.6 g
Cholesterol   131 mg
Sodium   262 mg

Ingredients

2 sweet potatoes, peeled and cubed
1 C. brown sugar
1/2 C. butter
1/2 C. milk
2 large eggs
1 tsp vanilla extract
1/3 C. butter, melted
1 C. chopped pecans
1/3 C. all-purpose flour

Directions

1. Coat a baking dish with nonstick spray or oil. Then set your oven to 375 degrees before doing anything else.
2. Boil the potatoes in water and salt for 23 mins. Remove all liquid and mash the potatoes.
3. Get a bowl and put in 3 C. of potatoes and the following: vanilla extract, brown sugar, eggs, half a C. of butter, and milk.
4. Mix with an electric mixer or by hand until very smooth.
5. Put everything your baking dish.
6. Get a 2nd bowl, mix: pecans, one third C. of melted butter, and flour.
7. Mix until smooth.
8. Then pour over the sweet potatoes in the baking dish.
9. Cook in the oven for 27 mins.
10. Enjoy.

Potatoes and Kielbasa

Prep Time: 20 mins
Total Time: 1 hr 50 mins

Servings per Recipe: 6
Calories   777 kcal
Fat   48.4 g
Carbohydrates   61.1g
Protein   25 g
Cholesterol   100 mg
Sodium   1415 mg

Ingredients

- 2 Kielbasa sausage rings, cut into 2-inch pieces
- 8 potatoes, peeled and quartered
- 1 onion, cut into chunks
- 1 (8 oz.) package baby carrots
- 4 cloves garlic, crushed
- salt and ground black pepper to taste
- 3 tbsps olive oil

Directions

1. Set your oven to 350 degrees before doing anything else.
2. Get a Dutch oven and combine in it: garlic, salt, kielbasa, pepper, carrots, olive oil, onions, and potatoes.
3. Cover the pan with some foil.
4. Cook everything in the oven for 1 hour.
5. Then cook for another 35 mins with no foil.
6. Enjoy.

ITALIAN STYLE
Beef and Veggies Pierogies Skillet

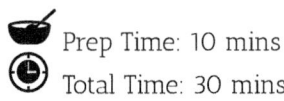

Prep Time: 10 mins
Total Time: 30 mins

Servings per Recipe: 4
Calories 417.7
Fat 22.6g
Cholesterol 91.9mg
Sodium 889.9mg
Carbohydrates 23.5g
Protein 30.6g

Ingredients

1 lb ground beef
1/2 C. onion, chopped
1/4 C. all-purpose flour
1 cans beef broth
1 packages frozen cheese and potato pierogies, thawed
2 C. frozen mixed vegetables, thawed and drained
1/2 tsp salt
1/2 tsp black pepper
1/2 tsp Italian seasoning
1/2 C. cheddar cheese, shredded

Directions

1. Place a large pan over medium heat: Brown in it the beef with onion for 8 min.
2. Discard the excess grease and reserve 3 tbsp of it only.
3. Add the flour to the beef mix and toss them to coat. Stir in the broth and cook them until they start boiling.
4. Let them cook for 2 to 3 min until the sauce thickens.
5. Add the seasonings with veggies and pierogies. Let them cook for 5 to 6 min. Top them with cheese then serve your skillet hot.
6. Enjoy.

Wonton Cheddar Pierogies

Prep Time: 1 hr
Total Time: 1 hr 15 mins

Servings per Recipe: 12
Calories   208.3
Fat   11.6g
Cholesterol   32.8mg
Sodium   258.6mg
Carbohydrates   21.6g
Protein   4.5g

Ingredients

42 wonton wrappers
2 large baking potatoes, diced and cooked
1/2 C. cheddar cheese, grated
2 tbsp butter
salt and pepper
water
flour
1/2 C. butter
1/4 C. onion, very finely diced

Directions

1. Place a large pan over medium heat: Mash in it the cheese with beef, a pinch of salt and pepper.
2. Place a wonton paper on a working surface. Place 1 tsp of the potato mixture in the middle of it.
3. Brush the edges with some water then fold it in half. Press the edges to seal them and place the pierogies on a greased baking sheet.
4. Repeat the process with the remaining ingredients.
5. Bring a large salted pot of water to a boil. Cook in it the pierogies for 4 min.
6. Place a large skillet over medium heat. Heat in it the butter. Stir in the onion with a pinch of salt and cook them for 4 min.
7. Serve your pierogies warm with the onion sauce.
8. Enjoy.

DOUBLE STUFFED
Pierogies

Prep Time: 30 mins
Total Time: 45 mins

Servings per Recipe: 4
Calories 550.1
Fat 16.7g
Cholesterol 166.8mg
Sodium 752.6mg
Carbohydrates 79.6g
Protein 19.5g

Ingredients

2 potatoes, cooked mashed
1 C. cottage cheese, drained
1 onion, minced and fried
1 egg yolk, beaten
1 tbsp butter, melted
1 tsp sugar
1/4 tsp salt
pepper, to taste
2 1/4 C. flour

1/2 tsp salt
2 tbsp butter
1 large egg
1 egg yolk
1/2 C. reduced-fat milk
2 tbsp sour cream
12 C. salt water

Directions

1. Get a large mixing bowl: Mix in it the mashed potato with cheese, onion egg yolk, butter, sugar and salt to make the filling.
2. Get a large mixing bowl: Mix in it all the dough ingredients until you get a smooth dough.
3. Cover it completely with kitchen towel and let it rest for 3 h.
4. Place the dough on a floured surface flatten it on a floured surface until it become thin.
5. Use a 3 inches cookie cutter to cut the dough into circles. Place 2 tbsp of the potato filling at one side of the dough circle.
6. Pull the other side over the filling and press it with a fork to seal the edges. Repeat the process with the remaining dough and filling.
7. Bring a large salted pot of water to a boil. Cook in it the pierogies in batches for 6 to 8 min.
8. Drain the pierogies then serve them with your favorite dipping sauce.
9. Enjoy.

The Brooklyn Style Sandwich

Prep Time: 30 mins
Total Time: 45 mins

Servings per Recipe: 4
Calories   892 kcal
Fat   45.3 g
Carbohydrates   79.5g
Protein   42.7 g
Cholesterol   97 mg
Sodium   1604 mg

Ingredients

- 3 C. shredded cabbage
- 2 tbsps vegetable oil
- 2 tbsps apple cider vinegar
- 2 tbsps white sugar
- 1 tsp adobo seasoning
- 1 tsp ground black pepper
- 4 C. vegetable oil for frying
- 3 whole russet potatoes
- 8 thick slices Italian bread
- 1 lb sliced pastrami (divided)
- 4 slices provolone cheese
- 8 slices tomato

Directions

1. Get a bowl and combine evenly: black pepper, cabbage, adobo, veggie oil (2 tbsps), sugar, and vinegar.
2. Get a large pot and get your oil to 375 degrees then set your oven to 225 degrees before doing anything else.
3. Dice your potatoes into slices and fry them in the oil for 6 mins.
4. Now place the potatoes to the side.
5. For 6 mins toast your bread in the oven.
6. On 4 slices of bread layer: pastrami and cheese.
7. Now toast the pieces for 4 more mins to melt the cheese.
8. Layer the following on the pastrami: 2 tomato pieces, cabbage mix, fried potatoes, and another piece of toasted bread.
9. Enjoy.

LATKES

Prep Time: 10 mins
Total Time: 20 mins

Servings per Recipe: 5
Calories	219 kcal
Fat	11 g
Carbohydrates	25.6 g
Protein	5.3 g
Cholesterol	74 mg
Sodium	731 mg

Ingredients

3 C. peeled and mashed baked potatoes
1 C. chopped white onion
1 tbsp minced garlic
1 1/2 tsps salt
1 tsp freshly ground multi-colored peppercorns

5 tbsps all-purpose flour
2 eggs, whisked
2 C. extra-virgin olive oil, or as need for frying

Directions

1. Get a deep fryer or Dutch oven heat your oil to 375 degrees.
2. Get a bowl, and mix: beaten eggs, potatoes, flour, garlic, ground peppercorns, salt, and onions.
3. Make sure to remove all chunks and lumps in your potato mixture.
4. Create some small baseball sized balls from the potatoes then flatten them out.
5. Fry each flattened piece of potato for 4 mins per side.
6. Then place them on some paper towel to remove excess oils.

Cranberries and Potatoes

Prep Time: 10 mins
Total Time: 55 mins

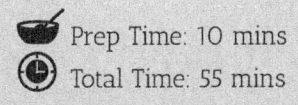

Servings per Recipe: 10
Calories   777 kcal
Fat   48.4 g
Carbohydrates   61.1g
Protein   25 g
Cholesterol   100 mg
Sodium   1415 mg

Ingredients

- 1 (12 oz.) package whole cranberries
- 1 small unpeeled orange, sliced
- 1 1/3 C. white sugar
- 1/2 C. pecan pieces
- 1/4 C. orange juice
- 3/4 tsp ground cinnamon
- 1/4 tsp ground nutmeg
- 1/8 tsp ground mace
- 1 (40 oz.) can cut yams, drained

Directions

1. Set your oven to 375 degree before doing anything else.
2. Get a bowl, and mix: mace, cranberries, nutmeg, orange slices, cinnamon, sugar, orange juice, pecans.
3. Enter everything into a casserole dish.
4. Cook in the oven for 35 mins. Add in your yams then cook for another 15 mins.

SUN
Skillet

🥣 Prep Time: 10 mins
🕐 Total Time: 25 mins

Servings per Recipe: 2
Calories 314.5
Fat 11.8g
Cholesterol 186.0mg
Sodium 666.9mg
Carbohydrates 42.0g
Protein 11.1g

Ingredients

2 potatoes, peeled, boiled and sliced
1 tbsp oil
2 eggs
1/2 C. onion, sliced
1/2 tsp salt
1 tsp pepper
1 tsp sumac

Directions

1. Place a pan over medium heat. Heat in it the oil. Cook in it the onion with potato for 5 min.
2. Get a mixing bowl: Whisk in it the eggs with a pinch of salt and pepper.
3. Spread the potato and onion in the pan. Pour the beaten eggs all over them.
4. Put on the lid and let the fritter cook until the egg sit then serve it warm.
5. Enjoy.

Baked Greek Potatoes

Prep Time: 20 mins
Total Time: 2 hrs 20 mins

Servings per Recipe: 4
Calories   418 kcal
Fat   18.5 g
Carbohydrates   58.6 g
Protein   7 g
Cholesterol   < 1 mg
Sodium   < 596 mg

Ingredients

- 1/3 C. olive oil
- 1 1/2 C. water
- 2 cloves garlic, finely chopped
- 1/4 C. fresh lemon juice
- 1 tsp dried thyme
- 1 tsp dried rosemary
- 2 cubes chicken bouillon
- ground black pepper to taste
- 6 potatoes, peeled and quartered

Directions

1. Set your oven to 350 degrees before doing anything else.
2. Get a bowl, combine: pepper, olive oil, bouillon, water, rosemary, water, thyme, garlic, and lemon juice.
3. Layer the potatoes in a casserole dish and top everything with the lemon mix.
4. Place some foil around the dish and cook the contents in the oven for 90 mins.
5. Flip the potatoes every 30 mins while cooking.
6. Enjoy.

MINTY
Potato Salad

Prep Time: 10 mins
Total Time: 35 mins

Servings per Recipe: 2
Calories	139.2
Fat	6.8g
Cholesterol	0.0mg
Sodium	152.7mg
Carbohydrates	17.7g
Protein	2.0g

Ingredients

200 g potatoes, peeled
1 tbsp olive oil
1 tbsp white vinegar
1 tsp dried mint
1/8 tsp salt, to taste

1/8 tsp ground black pepper, to taste

Directions

1. Slice the potatoes in small dices. Bring a salted pot of water to a boil then cook in it the potato until it becomes soft. Remove it from the water.
2. Toss the cooked potato with olive oil, white vinegar, dried mint, salt and black pepper. Place the salad in the fridge to lose heat for 1 h.
3. Enjoy.

Saucy Greens Potato Salad

Prep Time: 20 mins
Total Time: 45 mins

Servings per Recipe: 6
Calories   269.6
Fat   5.1g
Cholesterol   0.0mg
Sodium   238.9mg
Carbohydrates   52.4g
Protein   7.6g

Ingredients

- 3 onions cut into crescents
- 2 tbsp olive oil
- 1 1/2 lbs green beans
- 3 large ripe tomatoes cut into wedges
- 1 C tomato sauce
- 1 C water
- 3 large potatoes cut into chunks
- Salt and pepper

Directions

1. Place a skillet over medium heat and heat the oil in it.
2. Cook in it the onions for 3 to 5 min or until it becomes golden.
3. Stir in the rest of the ingredients then put on the lid and let them cook for 5 to 10 min or until they become soft.
4. Serve your warm veggies salad with your favorite toppings.
5. Enjoy.

ALGERIAN
Poached Eggs (Shakshouka II)

Prep Time: 1 hr 35 mins
Total Time: 3 hrs 35 mins

Servings per Recipe: 8
Calories   908.7
Fat   29.0g
Cholesterol   70.3mg
Sodium   473.1mg
Carbohydrates   125.0g
Protein   34.9g

Ingredients

- 1 yellow onion, chopped
- 8 lamb chops or 8 skinless chicken pieces
- 3 garlic cloves, chopped
- 2 medium carrots, sliced
- 2 medium zucchini, sliced
- 2 large potatoes, diced
- 1/4 swede or 1/4 turnip, diced
- 1 parsnip, diced
- 1 C. chickpeas, drained
- 2 tsp. ras el hanout spice mix
- salt & pepper
- 1 pinch dried mint
- 1 tbsp. sunflower oil or 1 tbsp. vegetable oil
- 1 C. of liquidized tomato puree
- 6 1/2 C. water
- 1 large green chili, roughly chopped

Directions

1. Place a large skillet over medium heat. Heat in it the oil.
2. Stir in it ras el hanout with meat. Cook them for 3 min.
3. Stir in the zucchini, with parsnip, carrot, potato, and swede.
4. Stir in 4 C. of water with chili pepper, a pinch of salt and pepper.
5. Put on the lid and lower the heat. Cook it for 42 min.
6. Stir in the chickpeas with dry mint, and 2 1/2 C. water. Cook it for an extra 32 min with the lid on.
7. Adjust the seasoning of your soup then serve it hot.
8. Enjoy.

Sweet Potato Casserole

Prep Time: 15 mins
Total Time: 40 mins

Servings per Recipe: 12
Calories   433 kcal
Fat   20.5 g
Carbohydrates   60.3g
Protein   4.1 g
Cholesterol   65 mg
Sodium   170 mg

Ingredients

2 (29 oz.) cans sweet potatoes in light syrup, drained
1/2 C. white sugar
1/2 C. butter, melted
2 eggs, beaten
1 tsp vanilla extract
1/3 C. milk
1/3 C. butter, melted

1 C. brown sugar
1/2 C. all-purpose flour
1 C. pecan halves

Directions

1. Set your oven to 350 degrees before doing anything else.
2. Put your potatoes in a bowl and mash them up nicely.
3. Then add in milk, sugar, vanilla, half a C. of melted butter, and eggs. Continue mixing until everything is nicely even.
4. Get a 2nd bowl, mix evenly: flour, 1/3 melted butter, pecans, and brown sugar.
5. Get a casserole dish and fill it with your mashed potatoes and then top the potatoes with your pecan mixture.
6. Cook in the oven for 27 mins.
7. Enjoy.

POTATOES and Garlic

Prep Time: 5 mins
Total Time: 1 hr 5mins

Servings per Recipe: 4
Calories   225 kcal
Fat   6.9 g
Carbohydrates   37.5g
Protein   4.4 g
Cholesterol   0 mg
Sodium   919 mg

Ingredients

4 medium baking potatoes, scrubbed
2 tbsps olive oil
2 tsps garlic salt, or to taste
salt and pepper to taste

Directions

1. Set your oven to 375 degrees before doing anything else.
2. Get a smaller bowl: add in olive oil.
3. Get a 2nd smaller bowl add in: pepper, and garlic salt.
4. Cover your potatoes with olive oil, by dipping, or rolling them in the bowl of oil. Then coat them with the dry seasonings.
5. Cook the potatoes for 1 hr in the oven directly on the rack.
6. Enjoy.

Sweet Potatoes II

Prep Time: 20 mins
Total Time: 1 hr 5 mins

Servings per Recipe: 7
Calories	449 kcal
Fat	21.7 g
Carbohydrates	61g
Protein	5.4 g
Cholesterol	84 mg
Sodium	315 mg

Ingredients

- 3 1/2 C. mashed sweet potatoes
- 1/4 C. milk
- 1/4 C. orange juice
- 2 eggs, beaten
- 1 tsp vanilla extract
- 1/2 C. white sugar
- 1/2 tsp salt
- 3 tbsps butter, softened
- 1/2 tsp ground nutmeg
- 1/2 tsp ground cinnamon
- 1/4 C. butter, softened
- 3/4 C. packed light brown sugar
- 1/2 C. all-purpose flour
- 3/4 C. chopped pecans

Directions

1. Coat a casserole dish with oil or nonstick spray. Then set your oven to 350 degrees before doing anything else.
2. Get a bowl, mix: cinnamon, potatoes, nutmeg, milk, butter, eggs, salt, vanilla, and sugar.
3. Enter this into your casserole dish.
4. Get a 2nd bowl, evenly mix: pecans, one fourth C. of butter, flour, and brown sugar.
5. Top your sweet potatoes with this mix.
6. Cook everything in the oven for 50 mins.
7. Enjoy.

BAKED
Potatoes Remix

Prep Time: 10 mins
Total Time: 1 hr 15 mins

Servings per Recipe: 4
Calories	321 kcal
Fat	7.3 g
Carbohydrates	61g
Protein	4.8 g
Cholesterol	0 mg
Sodium	92 mg

Ingredients

- 2 tbsps olive oil
- 3 large sweet potatoes
- 2 pinches dried oregano
- 2 pinches salt
- 2 pinches ground black pepper

Directions

1. Coat a casserole dish with olive oil. Then set your oven to 350 before doing anything else.
2. Clean and remove the skin from your potatoes.
3. Cut them into bit sized chunks.
4. Enter the potatoes in the casserole dish and stir them so they get coated with olive oil.
5. Season the potatoes with pepper, oregano, and salt.
6. Cook in the oven for 1 hr.
7. Enjoy.

Dip for Baked Potatoes

Prep Time: 10 mins
Total Time: 8 hrs 10 mins

Servings per Recipe: 16
Calories	125 kcal
Fat	11 g
Carbohydrates	2.2g
Protein	4.8 g
Cholesterol	32 mg
Sodium	326 mg

Ingredients

- 1 (8 oz.) package cream cheese, softened
- 1 (8 oz.) container sour cream
- 1 (1 oz.) package ranch dressing mix
- 3 green onions, thinly sliced
- 1 C. shredded Cheddar cheese
- 2/3 (3 oz.) can real bacon bits

Directions

1. Get a bowl, evenly mix: cheddar, ranch dressing mix, bacon bits, sour cream, green onions, and cream cheese.
2. Chill in the fridge for 8 hours.
3. Enjoy with some fried potatoes or any baked potato recipe.

MUSHROOM and Onion Baked Potato

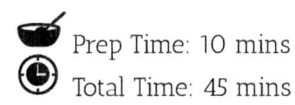

Prep Time: 10 mins
Total Time: 45 mins

Servings per Recipe: 1
Calories	427 kcal
Fat	12.1 g
Carbohydrates	71.7g
Protein	10.9 g
Cholesterol	31 mg
Sodium	438 mg

Ingredients

- 1 large baking potato
- 1 tbsp unsalted butter
- 1/4 C. chopped onions
- 1/2 C. chopped mushrooms
- salt to taste
- 2 tbsps nonfat plain yogurt

Directions

1. Set your oven to 450 degrees before doing anything else.
2. Get a fork and poke some holes into each potato.
3. For 10 min microwave the potatoes on high.
4. Then put all the potatoes in a casserole dish.
5. Cook them in the oven for 17 mins.
6. Meanwhile get a pan and cook your onions in melted butter until soft, then add in your mushrooms and stir fry for another 6 mins.
7. Add in your salt.
8. Before serving the potatoes cut an opening into each and place in some of the onions and mushrooms.
9. Enjoy.

Wedges one Right

Prep Time: 15 mins
Total Time: 45 mins

Servings per Recipe: 6
Calories   196 kcal
Fat   5 g
Carbohydrates   35.4g
Protein   4.3 g
Cholesterol   0 mg
Sodium   389 mg

Ingredients

- 6 red potatoes, cut into wedges
- 2 tbsps olive oil
- 2 tsps onion powder
- 2 tsps chili powder
- 1 tsp garlic powder
- 1 tsp garlic salt
- salt and ground black pepper to taste

Directions

1. Set your oven to 375 degrees before doing anything else.
2. Get a casserole dish and layer your potato wedges evenly.
3. Drizzle olive oil over them evenly as well.
4. Get a bowl and mix: garlic salt, onion powder, garlic powder, and chili powder.
5. Evenly coat the potatoes with your dry seasoning mixture.
6. Cook in the oven for 35 mins. Then add a bit more pepper and salt before serving.
7. Enjoy with some potato dip

CLASSIC
Cracked Potato and Beef Roast

Prep Time: 30 mins
Total Time: 2 hrs 30 mins

Servings per Recipe:	10
Calories	560.6
Fat	38.4 g
Cholesterol	125.2 mg
Sodium	356.8 mg
Carbohydrates	17 g
Protein	35 g

Ingredients

- 2 tbsp minced fresh rosemary
- 4 garlic cloves, minced
- 1 tsp salt
- 1 tsp dry mustard
- 1 tsp cracked black pepper
- 1 (4 lb) well-trimmed beef roast
- 2 tbsp vegetable oil
- 3 medium baking potatoes, quartered
- 2 large sweet potatoes, halved, quartered
- 4 small onions, halved

Directions

1. Before you do anything set the oven to 500 F.
2. Get a small bowl: Mix in it the rosemary, garlic, salt, mustard, and pepper. Rub half of the mix into the beef roast and place it aside.
3. Get a large mixing bowl: Toss in it the half of the remaining seasoning mix. Add the potatoes with onion and toss them well.
4. Transfer the roast to a rack in roasting pan with the fatty side facing up. Cook the roast in the oven for 25 min.
5. Arrange the veggies mix around the roast and cook them for 2 h. Cover the roast with a loose piece of foil and allow it to rest for 17 min.
6. Serve your beef roast and veggies warm.
7. Enjoy.

Italian Countryside Fries

Prep Time: 20 mins
Total Time: 55 mins

Servings per Recipe: 4
Calories   306.4
Fat   7.1g
Cholesterol   0.0mg
Sodium   19.7mg
Carbohydrates   55.8g
Protein   6.4g

Ingredients

6 medium potatoes, skin removed, sliced into fries
1 ounce Italian dressing
2 tablespoons oil

1 tablespoon fresh parsley, Chopped

Directions

1. Set your oven to 350 degrees before doing anything else.
2. Once your potatoes have been sliced pat them dry and let them sit for about 20 mins to dry out further.
3. Get a bowl and place your fries in it. Top the fries with the oil and stir everything.
4. Get a cookie sheet or casserole dish and place your fries into the dish or on the sheet. Top the fries evenly with the dressing mix and then toss everything. Then top the fries again with the parsley and toss again.
5. Cook the fries in the oven for 22 mins then turn the fries over.
6. Now continue to cook then for 4 to 8 more mins with an oven temperature of 450.
7. Enjoy.

HOT PEPPER
White Pepper French Fries

Prep Time: 5 mins
Total Time: 20 mins

Servings per Recipe: 5
Calories 257.2
Fat 3.0g
Cholesterol 0.0mg
Sodium 136.3mg
Carbohydrates 52.9g
Protein 6.1g

Ingredients

4 large potatoes, scrubbed, cut into strips
8 cups ice water
1 teaspoon garlic powder
1 teaspoon onion powder
1/4 teaspoon salt
1 teaspoon white pepper
1/4 teaspoon allspice
1 teaspoon hot pepper flakes
1 tablespoon vegetable oil

Directions

1. Get a bowl of cold water with some ice and submerge your potatoes in it. Place a covering of plastic on the bowl, and let the potatoes sit in the water for 2 hours.
2. Drain the potatoes from the water and pat them dry let them sit for about 15 to 20 mins.
3. Set your oven to 475 degrees before doing anything else.
4. Get a resealable plastic bag and add in the following spices then toss them together: pepper flakes, garlic and onion powder, allspice, salt, and white pepper. Once the spices have been tossed together evenly.
5. Add in your potatoes and toss everything. Coat your potatoes with some oil then place everything into a casserole dish that has been coated with nonstick spray.
6. Cover the dish with some foil and cook the potatoes for 17 mins in the oven. Discard the foil and continue to bake the fires for another 12 to 15 mins or until they are fully done.
7. Try to flip the fries at least twice during the baking process when there is no foil on the dish.
8. Enjoy.

English Salt & Vinegar Fries

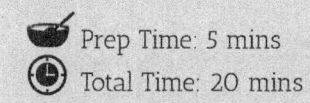

Prep Time: 5 mins
Total Time: 20 mins

Servings per Recipe: 4
Calories   156.1
Fat   3.6g
Cholesterol   0.0mg
Sodium   11.2mg
Carbohydrates   28.5g
Protein   2.6g

Ingredients

- 1 1/4 lbs baking potatoes, scrubbed, peeled, chopped into thin fries
- 3 cups water
- 2 tablespoons distilled white vinegar, plus 2 teaspoons distilled white vinegar, divided
- 1 tablespoon canola oil
- salt

Directions

1. Get a bowl and combine your 2 tbsp of white vinegar and the water. Stir the liquid then place your potatoes in it. Let the potatoes sit under water for at least 40 mins to 45 mins.
2. Now set your oven to 400 degrees before doing anything else.
3. Once the oven is hot drain your potatoes and pat them dry.
4. Get a 2nd bowl for your potatoes after they have been patted dry. Add in your canola oil to the bowl and stir the potatoes to evenly coat them.
5. Get a casserole dish or jelly roll pan and coat it with some nonstick spray. Evenly spread out your potatoes on the dish and once the oven is hot begin to cook them for 22 mins. Flip the potatoes by stirring everything and continue to bake them for about 7 to 11 more mins or until you find that they are completely done.
6. Remove the fries from the oven and let them cool slightly then mix the fries with two more tsps of vinegar and liberally with some salt according to your tastes.
7. Enjoy.

3-INGREDIENT French Fries

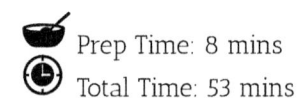

Prep Time: 8 mins
Total Time: 53 mins

Servings per Recipe: 2
Calories 283.3
Fat 13.6g
Cholesterol 0.0mg
Sodium 13.0mg
Carbohydrates 37.2g
Protein 4.3g

Ingredients

2 russet potatoes, cut into fries
2 tablespoons olive oil
2 tablespoons approximate sodium-free seasoning anything without salt

Directions

1. Set your oven to 350 degrees before doing anything else.
2. Place your fries into a bowl, and toss them with the olive oil. Once the potatoes have been evenly coated place them on a jelly roll pan evenly. Coat the pan with some nonstick spray. Top your fires with the 2 tbsps of seasoning and toss them well.
3. Cook the fries in the oven for about 35 to 45 mins. Flip them after about 25 to 30 mins.
4. Enjoy.

4-Ingredient Classicals

Prep Time: 10 mins
Total Time: 20 mins

Servings per Recipe: 1
Calories   584.1
Fat   8.3g
Cholesterol   15mg
Sodium   512.8mg
Carbohydrates   64.4g
Protein   7.4g

Ingredients

2 large potatoes, peeled, cut into matchsticks
1/4 teaspoon salt
oil for frying

1/4 cup of melted buttter

Directions

1. Get a bowl of water with ice. Place you cut potatoes into the bowl and let them sit submerged for 60 to 80 mins.
2. Drain all the excess liquid and begin to get your oil hot to 325 degrees. Working in sets fry your potatoes for 7 mins. Place the potatoes on a paper towel line plate to drain. Once the potatoes have dried a bit top them with the salt evenly, then the butter and toss everything together.
3. Enjoy.

PARMESAN
Onions and Fries

Prep Time: 10 mins
Total Time: 35 mins

Servings per Recipe: 4
Calories	253.6
Fat	0.3g
Cholesterol	0.0mg
Sodium	312.8mg
Carbohydrates	64.4g
Protein	7.4g

Ingredients

3 medium potatoes, sliced into thinner wedges
3 tablespoons butter or 3 tablespoons vegetable oil
1 - 2 tablespoon hot sauce, at room temperature
2 cups French's French fried onions, finely crushed
1/2 cup parmesan cheese, grated
1 C. ketchup, optional

Directions

1. Set your oven to 400 degrees before doing anything else.
2. Get a bowl, place your hot sauce, butter, and fries into the bowl and toss them evenly.
3. Get a 2nd bowl, combine your cheese and fried onions and work the mix evenly.
4. Coat your potatoes with the onion mix evenly by pressing the wedges into the mix then place everything into a casserole dish that has been coated with nonstick spray.
5. Cook everything in the oven for 24 mins then once the potatoes are done take them out the oven to cool.
6. Get a small bowl combine your ketchup and 2 tbsps of hot and stir everything together.
7. Top your fries with the ketchup sauce and toss them evenly.
8. Enjoy.

Cajun Spice Mix

Prep Time: 5 mins
Total Time: 5 mins

Servings per Recipe: 1
Calories   6 kcal
Fat   0.1 g
Carbohydrates   1.2g
Protein   0.2 g
Cholesterol   0 mg
Sodium   388 mg

Ingredients

- 2 tsps salt
- 2 tsps garlic powder
- 2 1/2 tsps paprika
- 1 tsp ground black pepper
- 1 tsp onion powder
- 1 tsp cayenne pepper
- 1 1/4 tsps dried oregano
- 1 1/4 tsps dried thyme
- 1/2 tsp red pepper flakes (optional)

Directions

1. Get a bowl, evenly mix or sift: red pepper flakes, salt, thyme, garlic powder, oregano, paprika, cayenne, onion powder, and black pepper.
2. Get a good container that is airtight and store your mix.

HOW TO BAKE
French Fries

🥣 Prep Time: 10 mins
🕐 Total Time: 40 mins

Servings per Recipe: 4
Calories   236 kcal
Fat   8.5 g
Carbohydrates   35g
Protein   6.2 g
Cholesterol   4 mg
Sodium   1833 mg

Ingredients

cooking spray
2 large potatoes, cut into 1/4-inch slices
2 tablespoons vegetable oil
1/4 cup grated Parmesan cheese
1 tablespoon garlic powder
1 tablespoon chopped fresh basil
1 tablespoon salt
1 tablespoon coarsely ground black pepper

Directions

1. Set your oven to 375 degrees before doing anything else.
2. Get a casserole dish and cover it with foil. Coat the foil with some nonstick spray then place your potatoes in a bowl.
3. Cover your potatoes with veggie oil and toss them then combine in the black pepper, parmesan, salt, basil, and garlic powder. Toss everything again to evenly coat the potatoes then layer them into the casserole dish evenly.
4. Cook everything in the oven for 31 to 36 mins or until the fries are golden.
5. Enjoy.

Louisiana
Creole Fries

Prep Time: 15 mins
Total Time: 1 hr

Servings per Recipe: 6
Calories   369 kcal
Fat   9.4 g
Carbohydrates   65.5g
Protein   7.7 g
Cholesterol   0 mg
Sodium   399 mg

Ingredients

1/4 cup olive oil
1 teaspoon garlic powder
1 teaspoon onion powder
1 teaspoon chili powder
1 teaspoon Cajun/Creole seasoning, see appendix
1 teaspoon sea salt

6 large baking potatoes, sliced into thin wedges

Directions

1. Set your oven to 400 degrees before doing anything else.
2. Get a bowl, combine: sea salt, olive oil, Cajun/creole spice, garlic powder, chili powder, and onion powder. Stir the spice together evenly then combine in the potatoes.
3. Toss everything together evenly then layer it all in a casserole dish spaced out evenly.
4. Cook the fries in the oven for about 30 to 37 mins then flip the potatoes and continue bake them for 8 more mins.
5. Enjoy.

COPYCAT FAST FOOD
Franchise Fries

Prep Time: 10 mins
Total Time: 1 hr 15 mins

Servings per Recipe: 4
Calories   600 kcal
Fat   322.4 g
Carbohydrates   394.8g
Protein   38.6 g
Cholesterol   0 mg
Sodium   112 mg

Ingredients

8 potatoes, peeled and cut into 1/4-inch thick fries
1/4 cup white sugar
2 tablespoons corn syrup
1 quart canola oil, or as needed
boiling water
sea salt to taste

Directions

1. Get a bowl, for your potatoes and let them sit submerged in water for 15 mins then remove the liquid and dry the potatoes.
2. Now submerge the potatoes in just enough boiling water then add in the corn syrup and sugar and stir everything. Do this in a metal bowl. Put everything in the fridge for 10 mins. Remove the liquid and dry the potatoes with some paper towels.
3. Get a casserole dish or jelly roll pan and lay out the fries on the dish, place a covering plastic on the dish and put everything in the freezer for 45 mins.
4. Now get your oil hot for frying to about 350 to 360 degrees and once the oil is hot begin to 1.3 of the fries in the oil for 3 mins. Place the fries on a plate with some paper towel to drain and let them for about 10 mins. Continue to work in batches until all the fries are done.
5. Now re fry the fries a second time 1/3 at a time for 6 mins each batch then season the fries with some salt.
6. Enjoy.

Russet Roast Stew

Prep Time: 20 mins
Total Time: 37 mins

Servings per Recipe: 6
Calories	165 kcal
Fat	3.6 g
Carbohydrates	23.8g
Protein	10.5 g
Cholesterol	18 mg
Sodium	390 mg

Ingredients

- 3 russet potatoes
- 2 C. 1/2-inch cubes roast beef
- 1 onion, finely chopped
- 1 green bell pepper, thinly sliced
- 1/2 C. sliced fresh mushrooms
- 1 tbsp vegetable oil

Directions

1. Make several holes in the potatoes with a fork and place them on an over proof plate. Microwave the potato for 9 min. Peel it and dice it.
2. Get a large bowl: Transfer the potato with beef and remaining veggies to it. Stir them.
3. Preheat a greased skillet. Lay in it the roast mix and cook them with stirring for 6 min. Turn over the mix and cook them for another 6 min.
4. Serve your stew warm.
5. Enjoy.

ONION SOUP
Roast

Prep Time: 25 mins
Total Time: 8 hrs 45 mins

Servings per Recipe: 8
Calories	310 kcal
Fat	12.5 g
Carbohydrates	22.3g
Protein	26.6 g
Cholesterol	71 mg
Sodium	952 mg

Ingredients

1 (3 lb) bottom round roast
ground black pepper to taste
garlic powder to taste
1 tbsp vegetable oil
2 (10.75 oz) cans condensed cream of mushroom soup
1 (1 oz) package dry onion soup mix
5 carrots, peeled and sliced into 1 inch pieces
6 small new potatoes, halved

Directions

1. Sprinkle the garlic powder with salt and pepper over the roast. Heat the oil in a large pot and place it over medium heat.
2. Cook in it the beef for 6 min for each side.
3. Get a mixing bowl: Add the mushroom and onion soup mix. Stir them well. Spread the mix in the bottom of a slow cooker. Place on it the carrot and potato followed by the roast.
4. Put on the lid and cook them for 7 h on low. Serve your roast warm.
5. Enjoy.

Potato Roast

🥣 Prep Time: 20 mins
🕒 Total Time: 4 hrs 20 mins

Servings per Recipe: 8
Calories   549 kcal
Fat   20.9 g
Carbohydrates   46 g
Protein   43.5 g
Cholesterol   124 mg
Sodium   277 mg

Ingredients

salt and pepper to taste
garlic powder to taste
6 lb pork butt roast
2 onion, sliced

20 new potatoes, raw
16 carrots, peeled
2 C. mushrooms, halved

Directions

1. Before you do anything set the oven to 350 F.
2. Place a large skillet over medium heat. Season the pork with some salt, pepper and garlic powder. Cook it in the pan for 5 min on each side.
3. Lay the pork butt in a large roasting pan then top it with the onion slices. Pour enough water in the pan to cover 3/4 of it. Put on the lid and cook it in the oven for 3 h 10 min.
4. Surround the roast with potato and carrots then roast them for 46 min. Add the mushroom on top and cook them for 17 min.
5. Place a piece of foil over the roast and allow it to rest for 12 min. Serve it warm.
6. Enjoy.

ROASTED Italian Cheesy Veggies

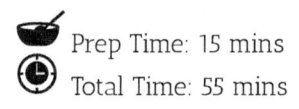

Prep Time: 15 mins
Total Time: 55 mins

Servings per Recipe: 6	
Calories	210 kcal
Fat	8.6 g
Carbohydrates	19.8g
Protein	13.4 g
Cholesterol	20 mg
Sodium	415 mg

Ingredients

2 russet potatoes, peeled and cut into 1-inch pieces
2 carrots, pared and cut into 1/2-inch slices
1 tbsp olive oil
1 tsp dried basil
1 tsp dried oregano
1/4 tsp salt
1/4 tsp black pepper

1 large zucchini, cut into 1/2-inch pieces
1 large red bell pepper, cut into 1/2-inch pieces
2 cloves garlic, minced
2 C. Shredded Reduced Fat 4 Cheese Italian Cheese
Fresh basil sprigs

Directions

1. Before you do anything set the oven to 400 F.
2. Toss the carrot with potato, a drizzle of olive oil, basil, oregano, salt and pepper in a large baking casserole.
3. Cook the veggies in the oven for 22 min. Add the bell pepper with garlic and zucchini then stir them. Cook them for another 22 min.
4. Toss the roasted veggies with cheese and bake them for 3 min. Serve your cheese roasted veggies warm.
5. Enjoy.

Smoked Feta Frittata

Prep Time: 15 mins
Total Time: 45 mins

Servings per Recipe: 6
Calories	303 kcal
Fat	17.8 g
Carbohydrates	16.1g
Protein	20.3 g
Cholesterol	399 mg
Sodium	530 mg

Ingredients

- 2 tbsp butter
- 2 C. chopped kale, or to taste
- 2 tbsp water
- 2 potatoes, cut into 1/4-inch slices
- 4 oz smoked salmon, finely chopped
- 1 tbsp capers
- 12 eggs, beaten
- 3 oz crumbled feta cheese

Directions

1. Preheat the oven broiler. Place the rack 6 inches away from the heat.
2. Place a large oven proof pan over medium heat. Cook in it the butter until it melts. Add the kale and cook it for 3 min.
3. Stir in the water and put on the lid. Place the lid aside and keep cooking the kale while stirring until no water is left.
4. Stir in the potatoes, salmon, and capers. Cook them for 4 min. Spread the mix in the pan and pour the eggs all over it to cover it.
5. Cook the mix for 6 min while stirring gently then spread it again to cover the bottom of the pan. Top it with cheese.
6. Cook it in the oven for 6 min. Serve your Frittata warm.
7. Enjoy.

CABBAGE
from Russia

Prep Time: 20 mins
Total Time: 1 hr 5 mins

Servings per Recipe: 8
Calories   128 kcal
Fat   5 g
Carbohydrates   19.8g
Protein   3 g
Cholesterol   11 mg
Sodium   908 mg

Ingredients

1 1/2 C. thinly sliced potatoes
1 C. thinly sliced beets
4 C. vegetable stock or water
2 tbsps butter
1 1/2 C. diced onions
1 tsp caraway seed (optional)
2 tsps salt
1 celery stalk, diced
1 large carrot, sliced
3 C. coarsely diced red cabbage

black pepper to taste
1/4 tsp fresh dill weed
1 tbsp cider vinegar
1 tbsp honey
1 C. tomato puree
sour cream, for topping
diced tomatoes, for garnish

Directions

1. Boil the following until soft in stock: beets and potatoes.
2. Get a frying pan and stir fry: salt, caraway, and onions.
3. Fry everything until the onions are see-through.
4. Now combine the following with the onions: cabbage, reserved stock, carrots, and celery.
5. Place a lid on the pan and cook the mix for 12 mins.
6. Combine the following with the cabbage: potatoes, beets, dill and pepper.
7. Stir the contents before adding: tomato puree, honey, and vinegar.
8. Place the lid back on the pan and lightly boil everything for 30 mins with a low to medium level of heat.
9. Place everything into a bowl, with a dollop of sour cream, diced tomatoes, and more dill.
10. Enjoy.

Maggie's Easy Cauliflower Soup (Vegetarian Approved)

Prep Time: 15 mins
Total Time: 50 mins

Servings per Recipe: 12
Calories	74 kcal
Fat	0.7 g
Carbohydrates	13.5g
Protein	4.6 g
Cholesterol	1 mg
Sodium	< 125 mg

Ingredients

- 1 tsp extra-virgin olive oil, or as needed
- 1/2 yellow onion, diced
- 1 leek, diced
- 3 cloves garlic, minced
- 1 head cauliflower, cut into florets
- 1/2 head broccoli, cut into florets
- 3 red potatoes, cut into bite-size pieces
- 1 (32 oz.) carton low-sodium vegetable broth
- water to cover
- 1 tbsp nutritional yeast, or more to taste
- 1/2 tsp ground turmeric
- 1 bay leaf
- salt and ground black pepper to taste
- 1 pinch cayenne pepper, or to taste
- 1 (12 fluid oz.) can fat-free evaporated milk
- 3 tbsps whole wheat flour, or as needed
- 1 tbsp curry powder

Directions

1. Stir fry your garlic, leeks, and onions in olive oil, in a large pot, for 6 mins.
2. Then add: potatoes, cauliflower, and broccoli.
3. Cook everything for 6 more mins.
4. Now pour in your broth and increase the heat.
5. Add some water as well to submerge all the veggies.
6. Season everything with: black pepper, curry, cayenne, turmeric, salt, and bay leaves then place a lid on the pot, ajar, and let the contents simmer for 27 mins.
7. Get a bowl, combine: flour, yeast, and milk. Then pour everything into the soup.
8. Let the soup simmer for 6 more mins.
9. Enjoy.

SAUCY Cabbage Beef Soup

Prep Time: 15 mins
Total Time: 35 mins

Servings per Recipe: 12
Calories 230 kcal
Fat 9.3 g
Carbohydrates 20.1g
Protein 14.2 g
Cholesterol 28 mg
Sodium 115 mg

Ingredients

1 tbsp vegetable oil
1 1/2 C. chopped onion
1 C. chopped celery
1 C. chopped carrots
2 cloves garlic, minced
10 C. beef stock
3/4 C. barley
1 bay leaf
3 sprigs fresh thyme, chopped

1/2 C. red wine
2 C. cubed potatoes
2 C. diced cooked beef
1 tsp browning sauce (optional)
1 1/2 C. chopped cabbage
Salt and pepper to taste

Directions

1. Heat the oil in a stock pot on medium heat. Add the garlic with celery, carrot and onion then them for 6 min.
2. Add the beef stock, barley, bay leaf and thyme. The soup on low until the barley becomes tender.
3. Stir in the wine, potatoes, and beef, browning and seasoning sauce.
4. The soup for 10 min
5. Stir in the cabbage and it for 14 min on low heat.
6. Adjust the seasoning of the soup then serve it warm.
7. Enjoy.

Golden Chuck Roast Soup

Prep Time:	20 mins
Total Time:	1 hr 20 mins
Servings per Recipe:	6
Calories	168 kcal
Fat	6.5 g
Carbohydrates	18.7 g
Protein	9.7 g
Cholesterol	17 mg
Sodium	383 mg

Ingredients

- 1/2 lb boneless beef chuck roast, cut into 1/2-inch pieces
- 1 tbsp olive oil
- 2 C. cubed unpeeled Yukon Gold potatoes
- 2 medium carrots, peeled, cut in half lengthwise and sliced
- 1 tbsp all-purpose flour
- 1 (32 oz.) carton Swanson(R) Lower Beef Broth
- 2 tbsp tomato paste
- 1 tsp chopped fresh thyme leaves
- 1 C. green beans, trimmed and cut into 1/2-inch pieces
- 1 C. frozen peas

Directions

1. Season the roast with some salt and pepper.
2. Place a large saucepan on medium heat and heat the oil in it. Brown in it the beef for 8 min.
3. Stir in the carrot with potato and them for 6 min. add the flour and mix them while cooking for 1 min.
4. Add the broth, tomato paste and thyme then bring them to a boil. Lower the heat and put on the lid then simmer the soup for 22 min. Stir in the rest of the ingredients and simmer the soup for another 22 min.
5. Adjust the seasoning of the soup then serve it warm.
6. Enjoy.

ITALIAN
Chunky Mushroom Soup

Prep Time: 20 mins
Total Time: 1 hr

Servings per Recipe: 10
Calories 404 kcal
Fat 23.5 g
Carbohydrates 28 g
Protein 20.8 g
Cholesterol 61 mg
Sodium 85 mg

Ingredients

2 lbs beef stew meat, diced into 1 inch pieces
Salt and pepper to taste
4 tbsp vegetable oil
1 C. chopped onion
1 C. sliced carrots
1/2 C. fresh sliced mushrooms
1/2 tsp minced garlic
1/4 tsp dried thyme

1 (14.5 oz.) can chicken broth
3 C. water
1 (16 oz.) package frozen mixed vegetables
4 small red potatoes cut into chunks
1/2 C. barley

Directions

1. Season the beef with some salt and pepper.
2. Place a large soup pot over medium heat. Heat in it half of the oil.
3. Add the beef and brown it for 6 min. Drain the beef and place it aside. Heat the remaining oil in the same pot.
4. Stir in the onions, carrots and mushrooms. Them for 6 min
5. Stir in the thyme with garlic and them for 4 min.
6. Add the chicken broth and 3 C. of water, mixed vegetables, potatoes and barley, a pinch of salt and pepper.
7. The soup until it starts boiling. Put on the lid and it on low heat for 1 h 35 min.
8. Adjust the seasoning of the soup then serve it warm.
9. Enjoy.

Chile Sauerkraut Soup

🍲 Prep Time: 30 mins
🕐 Total Time: 2 hrs 30 mins

Servings per Recipe: 6
Calories   177 kcal
Fat   6.7 g
Carbohydrates   27g
Protein   3.7 g
Cholesterol   4 mg
Sodium   513 mg

Ingredients

- 3 beef soup bones
- 2 tbsp olive oil, divided
- 1 (16 oz.) jar sauerkraut - rinsed and drained
- 1 onion, chopped
- 2 large baking potatoes, peeled and cubed
- 1 tbsp hot chile sauce, or to taste
- Salt to taste
- 1/4 C. sour cream (optional)

Directions

1. Put a large stew pot over medium heat. Add the bones and cover them with water 2 inches on top. Them until they start boiling. Lower the heat and them for 1 h. To make the stock.
2. Once the time is up, drain the bones and place them aside to cool down. Remove the meat in them and place it aside.
3. Place a large skillet over medium heat. Add the sauerkraut and it for 3 min. cover it with some water. Put on the lid and it for 32 min on low very low heat.
4. Discard the water and place the sauerkraut aside. Heat the rest of the oil in a large skillet. Add the onion and it for 4 min.
5. Stir the potato to the stock and bring it to a boil. Lower the heat and the potato for 14 min or until it become tender. Add the cooked onion with sauerkraut and the meat from the bones.
6. Stir in the chili sauce with a pinch of salt and pepper. Lower the heat and the soup for 16 min on low.
7. Adjust the seasoning of the soup then serve it warm.
8. Enjoy.

GREEN PEPPER
Sunday Hash

Prep Time: 10 mins
Total Time: 17 mins

Servings per Recipe: 2
Calories	331.6
Fat	21.4 g
Cholesterol	402.5 mg
Sodium	548.4 mg
Carbohydrates	19.3 g
Protein	15.9 g

Ingredients

1/2 C. chopped onion
1/2 C. chopped green pepper
2 tbsp butter
1 C. finely chopped cooked corned beef
1 C. finely chopped cooked potato
2/3 C. beef broth
Salt
Pepper
4 eggs

Directions

1. In a large pan, melt the butter on medium heat and sauté the onion till tender.
2. Stir in the corned beef, potato and broth and cook for about 3 minutes.
3. Stir in the salt and pepper.
4. With the back of a spoon, make 4 wells in hash.
5. Carefully, break 1 egg in each well.
6. Reduce the heat to low and cook, covered for about 4 minutes.

Tropical Mango Stew

Prep Time: 10 mins
Total Time: 40 mins

Servings per Recipe: 4
Calories	226.2
Fat	2.7g
Cholesterol	0.0mg
Sodium	25.1mg
Carbohydrates	43.9g
Protein	9.4g

Ingredients

- 1/2 tbsp canola oil
- 1 small onion, chopped
- 1 garlic clove, minced
- 1 medium sweet potato, peeled and diced
- 1 small red bell pepper, diced
- 3/4 lb tomatoes, diced
- 3/4 C. water
- 1 (16 oz.) cans black beans, well-rinsed and drained
- 1 mango, peeled, seeded and diced
- 1/8 C. chopped fresh cilantro
- salt, to taste (optional)

Directions

1. Place a large saucepan over medium heat. Heat the oil in it. Sauté in it the garlic with onion for 3 min.
2. Stir in the sweet potato, bell pepper, tomatoes, and water. Cook them until they start boiling. Lower the heat and put on the lid. Cook them for 16 min.
3. Stir in the beans and cook the stew for 5 min. Stir in the mango and cilantro and pinch of salt to taste. Serve your stew warm.
4. Enjoy.

EVERYTHING
Curry Dinner

Prep Time: 15 mins
Total Time: 1 hr 45 mins

Servings per Recipe: 6
Calories   625 kcal
Fat   23.5 g
Carbohydrates   70.7 g
Protein   35.4 g
Cholesterol   112 mg
Sodium   716 mg

Ingredients

1 (3 lb.) whole chicken
4 medium red potatoes, peeled and quartered
6 carrots, cut into 1/2 inch pieces
2/3 C. honey
1/3 C. Dijon mustard
3 tbsp butter
2 tbsp finely chopped onion
2 1/2 tsp curry powder
1/2 tsp salt
1/4 tsp red pepper flakes
1/4 tsp ground ginger
1/4 tsp finely chopped garlic
12 whole fresh mushrooms
2 apples, cored and quartered (optional)

Directions

1. Set your oven to 350 degrees F before doing anything else and arrange a rack in a roasting pan.
2. Arrange the chicken onto the rack in the roasting pan, breast side down.
3. Cook in the oven for about 1 hour.
4. Meanwhile in a pan, add the potatoes, carrots and enough water to cover and bring to a boil.
5. Cook for about 20 minutes.
6. In a pan, mix together the honey, mustard, butter, onion, curry powder, salt, cayenne pepper, ginger and garlic and bring to a boil, stirring continuously.
7. Remove from the heat and keep aside.
8. Drain the drippings from the roasting pan.
9. Place the potatoes, carrots, mushrooms and apples around the chicken evenly and drizzle with the honey mixture.
10. Cook in the oven for about 20 minutes.

Peanut Butter Coconut Curry

Prep Time: 20 mins
Total Time: 55 mins

Servings per Recipe: 4
Calories	690 kcal
Fat	41.2 g
Carbohydrates	47.3g
Protein	38.1 g
Cholesterol	73 mg
Sodium	1221 mg

Ingredients

- 2 tbsp vegetable oil
- 3 tbsp curry paste, see appendix
- 1 (3/4 inch thick) slice ginger, minced
- 1 1/4 lb. skinless, boneless chicken breast meat - cubed
- 3 tbsp brown sugar
- 3 tbsp fish sauce
- 3 tbsp tamarind paste
- 1/3 C. peanut butter
- 3 C. peeled, cubed potatoes
- 1 (13.5 oz.) can coconut milk
- 3 tbsp fresh lime juice

Directions

1. In a large pan, heat the vegetable oil on medium heat and sauté the curry paste and minced ginger for about 2 minutes.
2. Stir in the chicken cubes and cook for about 3 minutes.
3. Stir in the brown sugar, fish sauce, tamarind paste, peanut butter, potatoes and coconut milk and bring to a boil.
4. Reduce the heat to medium-low and simmer, covered for about 20 minutes.
5. Add the lime juice and cook for about 5 minutes.

JAMAICAN
Curry Chicken I

Prep Time: 20 mins
Total Time: 50 mins

Servings per Recipe: 6
Calories	348 kcal
Carbohydrates	13.8 g
Cholesterol	103 mg
Fat	20.3 g
Protein	27.8 g
Sodium	1353 mg

Ingredients

1/4 C. curry powder, divided
2 tbsps garlic powder
1 tbsp seasoned salt
1 tbsp onion powder
2 tsps salt
1 sprig fresh thyme, leaves stripped
1 pinch ground allspice, or more to taste
salt and ground black pepper to taste
2 1/4 lbs whole chicken, cut into pieces
3 tbsps vegetable oil
3 C. water
1 potato, diced
1/2 C. chopped carrots
2 scallions (green onions), chopped
1 (1 inch) piece fresh ginger root, minced
1 Scotch bonnet chili pepper, chopped, or to taste

Directions

1. Get a bowl and combine the following: pepper, 2 tbsps curry, salt, garlic powder, allspice, seasoned salt, thyme, onion powder.
2. Cover your chicken with the dry seasoning evenly.
3. Get a frying pan. Get 2 tbsps of curry and oil hot. Heat for 2 mins.
4. Mix in in chicken. Set heat to medium and combine carrot, water, potato, chili pepper, ginger, and scallions.
5. Place a lid on pan and let chicken simmer for 40 mins. Temp should be 165 degrees. Set chicken aside. Let the gravy get thicker if you like, by continuing to heat, otherwise serve.
6. Enjoy.

The Canadian Frittata

Prep Time: 10 mins
Total Time: 25 mins

Servings per Recipe: 2
Calories   340.7 kcal
Cholesterol   36.7mg
Sodium   968.8mg
Carbohydrates   25.7g
Protein   28.1g

Ingredients

- 1 tbsp olive oil
- 1 medium red skin white potato, washed
- 1/2 medium red bell pepper, chopped
- 3 green onions, washed and sliced
- 1/2 C. sliced mushrooms
- 3 slices Canadian bacon, chopped
- 1 C. egg substitute or 4 eggs, beaten with
- 1/4 C. milk
- 1/4 C. shredded mozzarella cheese
- salt and pepper

Directions

1. Grate your potatoes then begin to stir fry them with the bacon, bell peppers, mushrooms, and green onions, in olive oil.
2. Once the veggies are crispy and the potatoes have browned stir in some pepper, and salt.
3. Now top everything with the eggs and fry the mix for about 6 mins.
4. Lift the edge of the frittata to let the loose eggs run onto the pan.
5. Once the bottom of the frittata is completely set flip it.
6. Invert the pan over a plate and place the frittata back into the pan.
7. Cook the opposite side for about 2 mins then top everything with your cheese.
8. Shut the heat and place a lid on the pot.
9. Let the cheese melt then place the frittata on a serving dish.
10. Slice the frittata into two pieces then serve.
11. Enjoy.

TOMATO and Potato Frittata

Prep Time: 15 mins
Total Time: 45 mins

Servings per Recipe: 8
Calories   218.3 kcal
Cholesterol   213.3mg
Sodium   416.3mg
Carbohydrates   7.2g
Protein   13.5g

Ingredients

1 (9 5/8 oz.) packages pork sausage, crumbles
2 C. red potatoes, cubed and cooked
8 eggs
1/4 C. parmesan cheese, shredded
1/4 tsp salt
1/4 tsp ground black pepper
1/2 C. tomatoes, seeded and chopped
2 green onions, thinly sliced

Directions

1. For 5 mins stir fry your sausage then combine in the potatoes.
2. Get a bowl, combine: pepper, eggs, salt, and cheese.
3. Beat the mix until it is smooth then add everything to the potatoes.
4. Let the mix cook for 3 mins with a high level of heat then set the heat to low and place a lid on the pot.
5. Let the frittata cook for 15 mins then add a topping of onions and tomatoes.
6. Enjoy.

The Classical Morning Frittata

Prep Time: 10 mins
Total Time: 30 mins

Servings per Recipe: 6
Calories	630.1 kcal
Cholesterol	303.7mg
Sodium	1826.5mg
Carbohydrates	17.6g
Protein	27.9g

Ingredients

- 1 lb Jimmy Dean sausage
- 6 eggs
- 3 C. potatoes, chopped
- 1/4 C. onion
- 2 tbsps bell peppers, chopped
- 2 tbsps sweet red peppers, chopped
- 4 oz. monterey jack pepper cheese, chopped
- 4 oz. sharp cheddar cheese, shredded
- 2 tsps salt
- 2 tbsps half-and-half
- 2 tsps hot sauce
- 1/2 tsp baking soda
- 2 tsps pepper
- 2 tbsps olive oil

Directions

1. Set your oven to 350 degrees before doing anything else.
2. Fry your sausages then place them to the side.
3. Now fry your potatoes until they are brown, in oil, in a frying pan, then combine in the chopped pepper and onions.
4. Cook the mix until the onions are see-through.
5. Get a bowl and whisk your eggs then add in the baking soda, hot sauce, and half and half.
6. Add the eggs to the sausage mix in the pan then add your pepper jack cheese after dicing it then top everything with pepper and salt.
7. Top the mix further with the shredded cheddar and let the bottom of the frittata set in the pan.
8. Now place everything into the oven for 15 mins.
9. Enjoy.

CHEESY Beef & Potato Casserole

Prep Time: 20 mins
Total Time: 50 mins

Servings per Recipe: 6
Calories 241.6
Fat 14.8g
Cholesterol 77.3mg
Sodium 486.7mg
Carbohydrates 14.5g
Protein 12.4g

Ingredients

1 lb potato, peeled, boiled until tender
2 tbsps butter
1 tsp salt
2 tsps olive oil
1 small onion, finely chopped
1/2 lb ground beef

1/4 tsp pepper
1 medium egg, beaten
2 oz. gruyere cheese, grated

Directions

1. Set your oven to 350 degrees F before doing anything else and grease a casserole dish.
2. In a bowl, add the boiled potatoes, butter and salt and mash completely.
3. Heat a skillet and stir fry the beef, onion and pepper for about 5 minutes.
4. Drain the excess liquid and fat from the beef mixture.
5. Place the half of the potato mixture in the bottom of prepared casserole dish evenly.
6. Place the beef mixture and then topped with the remaining potato mixture evenly.
7. With the back of a spatula, smooth the surface of the potato mixture.
8. Brush the top of the potato mixture with the beaten egg and sprinkle with the cheese evenly.
9. Cook in the oven for about 30 minutes.

Veggie Scrambled Eggs

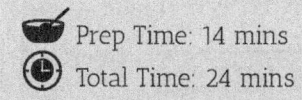

Prep Time: 14 mins
Total Time: 24 mins

Servings per Recipe: 3
Calories   464.1
Fat   10.8g
Cholesterol   423.0mg
Sodium   170.0mg
Carbohydrates   71.5g
Protein   21.3g

Ingredients

2 green peppers, cleaned and cut into strips
2 medium onions, sliced
4 roma tomatoes, sliced into 1/3s
5 red potatoes, washed, unpeeled and sliced
olive oil
salt and pepper
cayenne pepper
6 eggs

Directions

1. In a skillet, heat the oil on low heat and cook the onion, peppers, potatoes and spices till tender.
2. Stir in the tomatoes and increase the heat to medium.
3. In a bowl, beat the eggs and place them in the skillet.
4. Cook, stirring continuously, till the desired doneness of scramble.

HERBED Sweet Potato Frittata

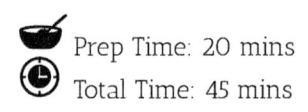

🥣 Prep Time: 20 mins
⏱ Total Time: 45 mins

Servings per Recipe: 8
Calories 207 kcal
Fat 17.1 g
Carbohydrates 4.4g
Protein 8.8 g
Cholesterol 208 mg
Sodium 401 mg

Ingredients

- 3 tbsp olive oil
- 1 small red onion, chopped
- 3 cloves garlic, chopped
- 2 green bell peppers, diced
- 12 eggs, beaten
- 1/2 C. chopped fresh basil leaves
- 4 sprigs fresh rosemary, leaves removed and chopped
- 1 tsp salt
- 1/2 tsp freshly ground black pepper
- 1 C. olive oil for frying
- 1 sweet potato, peeled and cut into thin matchsticks

Directions

1. Before you do anything preheat the oven to 350 F. Coat a casserole dish with a cooking spray.
2. Place a large oven proof over medium heat. Heat 3 tbsp of olive oil in it.
3. Add the onion with garlic and cook them for 6 min. Add the peppers and cook them for another 6 min. Stir in the eggs with basil, rosemary, salt, and pepper.
4. Lower the heat and cook the Frittata for 12 min. Place the Frittata in the oven for 16 min.
5. Heat 1 C. of olive oil in a large skillet or frying pan until it starts sizzling. Cook in it the sweet potato until it becomes golden brown.
6. Serve your sweet potato fried with the Frittata.
7. Enjoy.

Balsamic Roasted Veggies

Prep Time: 25 mins
Total Time: 1 hr 45 mins

Servings per Recipe: 4
Calories	1047 kcal
Fat	55.2 g
Carbohydrates	82.3g
Protein	51.2 g
Cholesterol	161 mg
Sodium	763 mg

Ingredients

- cooking spray
- 4 beets, peeled and cut into 3/4-inch cubes
- 2 new potatoes, peeled and cut into 3/4-inch cubes
- 2 parsnips, peeled and cut into 3/4-inch cubes
- 2 turnips, peeled and cut into 3/4-inch cubes
- 1 rutabaga, peeled and cut into 3/4-inch cubes
- 2 tbsp olive oil
- salt and ground black pepper to taste
- 1/3 C. vegetable broth
- 2 tbsp balsamic vinegar
- 1 pinch Italian seasoning, or to taste (optional)
- 1 (4 oz) package goat cheese, crumble

Directions

1. Before you do anything set the oven to 450 F. Grease a baking pan with a cooking spray.
2. Get a large bowl: Mix in it the beets, potatoes, parsnips, turnips, and rutabaga with olive oil, salt, and pepper. Lay the mix on the baking pan.
3. Cook the veggies on the oven for 42 min.
4. Get a small bowl: Whisk the broth, balsamic vinegar, and Italian seasoning. Drizzle the mix all over roasted veggies then cook them for 12 min.
5. Toss the roasted veggies with goat cheese warm.
6. Enjoy.

ZESTY
Veggies Roast

🥣 Prep Time: 45 mins
🕐 Total Time: 2 hrs 15 mins

Servings per Recipe: 8
Calories	297 kcal
Fat	4.2 g
Carbohydrates	64.7g
Protein	6 g
Cholesterol	0 mg
Sodium	103 mg

Ingredients

- 1 large butternut squash - peeled, seeded, and cut into 1-inch pieces
- 1 large delicata squash - peeled, seeded, and cut into 1-inch pieces
- 3 sweet potatoes, peeled and cut into 1-inch pieces
- 1 (2 lb) rutabaga, peeled and cut into 1-inch pieces
- 2 red potatoes, peeled and cut into 1-inch pieces
- 2 carrots, sliced
- 1 large onion, sliced
- 2 tbsp dried rosemary
- 2 tbsp dried thyme
- 1 tsp dried oregano
- 2 tbsp extra-virgin olive oil
- 6 dried bay leaves
- 1 dash lemon juice
- 1 dash apple cider vinegar
- 1 pinch salt
- 1 pinch ground black pepper

Directions

1. Before you do anything set the oven to 400 F. Coat a roasting dish with some oil or cooking spray.
2. Get a large bowl: Toss the butternut squash, delicata squash, sweet potato, rutabaga, and red potato pieces, carrots, and onion.
3. Get a small bowl: Stir in it the thyme with oregano and rosemary. Toss the veggies with the herbs mix and olive oil. Spread the veggies in the roasting dish.
4. Top them with vinegar, lemon juice and bay leaves, a pinch of salt and pepper. Cook the veggies in the oven for 1 h 32 min while stirring them 3 time. Serve your veggies warm.
5. Enjoy.

Cherry Potato Roast Salad

Prep Time: 15 mins
Total Time: 1 hr 30 mins

Servings per Recipe: 6
Calories	289 kcal
Fat	9.1 g
Carbohydrates	47.3g
Protein	8.6 g
Cholesterol	0 mg
Sodium	58 mg

Ingredients

- 12 new potatoes, halved
- 2 large red onions, each cut into 8 wedges
- 2 large yellow bell peppers, seeded and cubed
- 4 cloves garlic, peeled
- 1 eggplant, thickly sliced (optional)
- 1 tsp chopped fresh rosemary
- 2 tsps chopped fresh thyme
- 2 tbsp olive oil
- salt to taste
- 1 pint cherry tomatoes, halved
- 1/3 C. toasted pine nuts
- 1 (10 oz) bag baby spinach leaves
- 2 tbsp balsamic vinegar

Directions

1. Before you do anything set the oven to 400 F. Cover a baking pan with a large piece of foil.
2. Lay the potato in a ovenproof plate and microwave it for 5 min until it becomes soft.
3. Get a large bowl: Toss the cooked potato with onion, bell pepper, garlic, and eggplant, rosemary, thyme, and olive oil, a pinch of salt and pepper.
4. Transfer the veggies mix to the baking pan. Cook them in the oven for 37 min. Add the cherry tomatoes and cook them for 17 min.
5. Get a large bowl: Add the roasted veggies with spinach, vinegar and pine nuts. Stir them well and serve them.
6. Enjoy.

VEGETARIAN
Curry Japanese Style

Prep Time: 30 mins
Total Time: 1 hr

Servings per Recipe: 2
Calories	297 kcal
Fat	11.6 g
Carbohydrates	45.1g
Protein	8 g
Cholesterol	0 mg
Sodium	236 mg

Ingredients

2 C. cubed Japanese turnips
1 potato, peeled and cubed
1 tomato, diced
1 C. water
1/4 tsp ground turmeric
Spice Paste:
1 tsp canola oil
2 dried red chilis
2 small Thai green chilis
1 (1/2 inch) piece cinnamon stick
4 pearl onions
2 tbsp unsweetened dried coconut
1 tbsp coriander seeds
5 cashews
2 green cardamom pods
2 whole cloves

1/2 tsp fennel seeds
1/4 tsp cumin seeds
2 tbsp chopped cilantro
2 tbsp chopped fresh mint
1 tsp water, or as needed
1 tsp canola oil
1/2 tsp fennel seeds
1 (1 inch) piece cinnamon stick
2 cloves garlic, minced
1 (1 inch) piece fresh ginger root, minced
4 fresh curry leaves
1/4 C. peas
1 pinch salt

Directions

1. In a large pan, add the turnips, potato, diced tomato, 1 C. of the water and turmeric and bring to a boil.
2. Reduce the heat and simmer for about 15 minutes.
3. In a skillet, heat 1 tsp of the canola oil on medium heat and sauté the chilis, 1/2-inch piece of the cinnamon stick, pearl onions, coconut, coriander, cashews, cardamom pods, cloves, 1/2 tsp of the fennel seeds and cumin seeds for about 3 minutes.
4. Remove from the heat and transfer into a spice grinder.
5. Add the cilantro, mint and 1 tsp of the water and grind till a smooth paste forms.

6. In a large skillet, heat 1 tsp of the canola oil on medium-low heat and sauté 1/2 tsp of the fennel seeds and 1-inch piece of the cinnamon stick for about 30 seconds.
7. Add the minced garlic, ginger and curry leaves and sauté for about 2 minutes.
8. Add the cooked vegetables and spice paste and bring to a boil. (Add more water if curry becomes too thick.)
9. Stir in the green peas and salt.
10. Reduce the heat and simmer for about 10 minutes.

DUBLIN Dumplings

Prep Time: 30 mins
Total Time: 4 hrs 30 mins

Servings per Recipe: 6
Calories   595 kcal
Fat   9.2 g
Carbohydrates   94.4g
Protein   33.9 g
Cholesterol   58 mg
Sodium   2402 mg

Ingredients

2 (10.75 oz) cans condensed cream of chicken soup
3 C. water
1 C. chopped celery
2 onions, quartered
1 tsp salt
1/2 tsp poultry seasoning
1/2 tsp ground black pepper
4 skinless, boneless chicken breast halves
5 carrots, sliced
1 (10 oz) package frozen green peas
4 potatoes, quartered
3 C. baking mix
1 1/3 C. milk

Directions

1. Place a large pot over medium heat. Stir in it the soup, water, chicken, celery, onion, salt, poultry seasoning, and pepper. Put on the lid and cook them for 1 h 35 min over low heat.
2. Stir in the carrot with potato. Put on the lid and simmer them for 35 min.
3. Drain the chicken from the soup and shred it. Stir the chicken with pea back into the pot. Cook them for 6 min.
4. Get a mixing bowl: Mix in it the baking mix with milk and a pinch of salt until they make a soft dough. Spoon the dough over the stew.
5. Put on the lid and cook the stew for 1 h 40 min over low heat. Serve your stew hot.
6. Enjoy.

Turkey Stew with Buttermilk Dumplings

Prep Time: 10 mins
Total Time: 4 hrs 10 mins

Servings per Recipe: 4
Calories   449 kcal
Fat   22.4 g
Carbohydrates   38.2 g
Protein   23.3 g
Cholesterol   70 mg
Sodium   1961 mg

Ingredients

2 (10.75 oz) cans condensed cream of chicken soup
1 (15 oz) can chicken broth
1 1/2 C. chopped cooked turkey, or more to taste
1 C. chopped potatoes, or more to taste
1 C. chopped carrots, or more to taste
1/2 onion, chopped
2 tbsp butter
1 pinch garlic powder
1 pinch poultry seasoning
1/2 (10 oz) can refrigerated buttermilk biscuit dough, cut into squares

Directions

1. Grease a slow cooker: Stir in it the cream of chicken soup, chicken broth, turkey, potatoes, carrots, onion, butter, garlic powder, and poultry seasoning.
2. Put on the lid and cook the stew for 3 h on high. Dump the biscuits on top of the stew. Put on the lid and cook them for 1 h on high.
3. Serve your stew warm.
4. Enjoy.

BAKED
Golden Chicken and Potato

Prep Time: 30 mins
Total Time: 1 hr 10 mins

Servings per Recipe: 6
Calories	423 kcal
Fat	18.9 g
Carbohydrates	33.8g
Protein	28.7 g
Cholesterol	81 mg
Sodium	161 mg

Ingredients

- 1 serving cooking spray
- 2 sweet potatoes, sliced very thinly
- 2 Yukon Gold potatoes, sliced
- 1 large onion, sliced
- 1 (2 to 3 lb) roasting chicken
- 2 tbsp olive oil, or to taste
- 1 pinch salt and ground black pepper to taste

Directions

1. Before you do anything set the oven to 400 F. Spray some cooking spray on a roasting pan and place it aside.
2. Place the sweet potato slices followed by golden potato and onion in the roasting pan.
3. Put the chicken on top with its breast facing down. Make a large cut alone the chicken backbone and remove it then press it open in the shape of a butterfly.
4. Drizzle the olive oil on the chicken and sprinkle on it some salt and pepper then place it with the breast facing down on the veggies.
5. Cook the chicken and potato in the oven for 1 h 10 min. Allow the potato and chicken roast to rest for 12 min then serve them warm.
6. Enjoy.

Authentic New England Style Clam Chowder

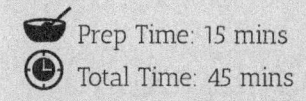

Prep Time: 15 mins
Total Time: 45 mins

Servings per Recipe: 8
Calories   396 kcal
Fat   22.5 g
Carbohydrates   24g
Protein   24.1 g
Cholesterol   101 mg
Sodium   706 mg

Ingredients

4 bacon turkey slices, chopped
1 1/2 C. onion, chopped
4 C. potatoes, peeled and cubed
1 1/2 C. water
Salt and freshly ground black pepper, to taste
3 tbsps butter
3 C. half-and-half

2 (10-oz.) cans minced clams, drained, reserving 1/2 C. of liquid

Directions

1. Heat a large nonstick soup pan on medium-high heat.
2. Add the bacon and cook for about 8-10 minutes.
3. Transfer the bacon into a bowl, leaving the fats in pan.
4. Add the onion and sauté for about 4-5 minutes with medium heat.
5. Add the potatoes and water and bring to a boil.
6. Cook, uncovered for about 15 minutes or till tender enough.
7. Stir in the butter and half-and-half.
8. Add clams with reserved liquid and stir to combine.
9. Cook, stirring occasionally, for about 5 minutes.
10. Serve hot with a topping of bacon.

POTATOES, Corn, and Steak Soup

Prep Time: 45 mins
Total Time: 2 hrs 15 mins

Servings per Recipe: 8
Calories 361 kcal
Fat 12.9 g
Cholesterol 84 mg
Sodium 1118 mg
Carbohydrates 26.9 g
Protein 36 g

Ingredients

2 tbsps butter
2 tbsps vegetable oil
1 1/2 lbs lean boneless beef round steak, cut into cubes
1/2 C. chopped onion
3 tbsps all-purpose flour
1 tbsp paprika
1 tsp salt
1/4 tsp ground black pepper
4 C. beef broth
2 C. water
4 sprigs fresh parsley, chopped
2 tbsps chopped celery leaves
1 bay leaf
1/2 tsp dried marjoram
1 1/2 C. peeled, minced Yukon Gold potatoes
1 1/2 C. sliced carrots
1 1/2 C. chopped celery
1 (6 oz.) can tomato paste
1 (15.25 oz.) can whole kernel corn, drained

Directions

1. Cook steak cubes and onion in a hot mixture of butter and oil for 10 minutes before stirring in a mixture of pepper, paprika, flour and salt into the pan.
2. Now add this mixture to a large pot containing a mixture of beef broth, water, celery leaves, marjoram, bay leave and parsley before cooking it for 45 minutes or until the meat is tender.
3. Now stir in potatoes, tomato paste, carrots, celery and corn before cooking it over low heat for 20 more minutes or until the vegetables are tender.
4. Remove bay leaf from the soup and serve.

Turkey Leg Soup

Prep Time: 15 mins
Total Time: 1 hr 25 mins

Servings per Recipe: 7
Calories	472 kcal
Fat	25.2 g
Cholesterol	146 mg
Sodium	1505 mg
Carbohydrates	24.6 g
Protein	37.1 g

Ingredients

- 2 turkey legs
- 1 C. minced celery
- 1 1/2 C. minced potatoes
- 2 (10.75 oz.) cans condensed cream of chicken soup
- 1 lb processed cheese, cubed
- 1 C. minced carrots
- 1 C. minced onion
- 1 (16 oz.) package frozen chopped broccoli
- 4 C. water

Directions

1. Bring water to boil after adding turkey and cook until tender before cutting up meat and adding it back into the pot.
2. Stir in onions, celery, potatoes and carrots, and cook until tender before adding frozen vegetables and cooking all this again for 15 minutes.
3. Add cream of chicken soup and also some cubed cheese, and cook until the cheese melts.
4. Serve.

PIEROGI
Milanese

Prep Time: 5 mins
Total Time: 5 hrs 5 mins

Servings per Recipe: 5
Calories	73.4
Fat	3.0g
Cholesterol	0.0mg
Sodium	341.6mg
Carbohydrates	11.9g
Protein	1.6g

Ingredients

- 1 cans crushed tomatoes
- 1 shallot, sliced
- 1 C. chopped green bell pepper
- 1 tbsp olive oil
- 1/2 tbsp red wine vinegar
- 1/2-1 tsp dried Italian seasoning
- black pepper
- 1 lb potato-filled pierogi, fresh or frozen

Directions

1. Stir the crushed tomatoes, shallots, peppers, oil, vinegar, Italian seasoning and black pepper in a slow cooker.
2. Put on the lid and cook them for 7 h on low or 4 on high.
3. Stir in the pierogies and put on the lid. Cook them for 1 h on low. Serve them warm.
4. Enjoy.

6-Ingredient Pierogies

Prep Time: 15 mins
Total Time: 1 hr

Servings per Recipe: 4
Calories   246.7
Fat   10.9 g
Cholesterol   65.0 mg
Sodium   647.3 mg
Carbohydrates   13.0 g
Protein   23.4 g

Ingredients

1 dozen frozen potato & cheese pierogi, thawed
1 cans cream of chicken soup
3/4 C. milk
1 cans sliced mushrooms, drained
1 C. frozen peas
2 C. cubed cooked chicken

Directions

1. Before you do anything, preheat the oven to 350 F.
2. Grease a baking dish with some butter. Lay in it the pierogies and place it aside.
3. Get a large mixing bowl: Whisk in it the soup, milk, mushrooms, peas, chicken, a pinch of salt and pepper.
4. Pour the mixture all over the pierogies. Place the casserole in the oven and let it cook for 48 min. Serve it hot.
5. Enjoy.

WHITE TUNA
Pierogi Bake

Prep Time: 15 mins
Total Time: 1 hr 15 mins

Servings per Recipe: 6
Calories   155.6
Fat   6.0g
Cholesterol   31.7mg
Sodium   427.0mg
Carbohydrates   2.8g
Protein   21.1g

Ingredients

24 frozen potato and cheddar pierogies
2 tsp canola oil
2 celery ribs, chopped
1 medium onion, chopped
2 cans tuna in water, drained
2 cans cream of mushroom soup
1 tbsp reduced-fat mayonnaise
6 slices low-fat cheddar cheese

Directions

1. Before you do anything, preheat the oven to 350 F. Grease a baking pan with some butter.
2. Cook the pierogies by following the instructions on the package.
3. Place a large pan over medium heat: Heat the oil in it. Sauté in it the onion with celery for 6 min.
4. Mix in the tuna with mayonnaise, soup, a pinch of salt and pepper. Cook them for 2 min.
5. Place the pierogies in the greased pan. Spread the tuna mixture all over it. Place the pan in the oven and bake it for 46 min.
6. Top the tuna casserole with cheese and bake it for an extra 3 min. Serve it hot.
7. Enjoy.

Pierogi Tortilla

Prep Time: 5 mins
Total Time: 10 mins

Servings per Recipe: 1
Calories	530.8
Fat	28.5g
Cholesterol	36.1mg
Sodium	931.4mg
Carbohydrates	52.6g
Protein	17.3g

Ingredients

- 1 small potato, thinly sliced
- 1 flour tortilla
- 1 tbsp crushed red pepper flakes
- 1/4 C. shredded Monterey Jack cheese
- 1/4 C. shredded Cheddar cheese
- 2 1/4 tsp Italian dressing
- 2 tsp olive oil
- 1 tsp basil
- salt
- pepper
- salsa
- sour cream
- guacamole

Directions

1. Place a large pan over medium heat: Heat the oil in it.
2. Add to it the potato slices with basil, a pinch of salt and pepper. Cook them for 4 to 6 min until they become soft.
3. Drain them and place them aside. Lay the tortilla in the hot pan.
4. Get a large mixing bowl: Mix in it the shredded cheese.
5. Sprinkle it over the tortilla then top it with the cooked potato, red peppers, Italian seasoning, a pinch of salt and pepper.
6. Fold the tortilla gently in half then serve it hot right away.
7. Enjoy.

SWEET and Salty Dumplings

🥣 Prep Time: 1 hr
🕐 Total Time: 1 hr 20 mins

Servings per Recipe: 10
Calories 650.7
Fat 19.5g
Cholesterol 78.1mg
Sodium 101.4mg
Carbohydrates 108.9g
Protein 12.0g

Ingredients

8 potatoes, peeled and cubed
1 egg
5 C. all-purpose flour
10 firm ripe peaches
1 C. brown sugar

1/2 C. butter, melted
1 C. heavy cream

Directions

1. Bring a large salted pot of water to a boil. Cook in it the potatoes until they become soft.
2. Drain the potatoes from the water and peel them. Mash them until they become smooth.
3. Get a large mixing bowl: Place in it the mashed potato with egg. Add to them the flour gradually while mixing them with your hand.
4. Cover the dough and let it rest for 2 min.
5. Place half of the dough on a floured surface. Roll it until it becomes 1/4 inch thick.
6. Slice it into 8 inches squares. Repeat the process with the other half of dough.
7. Place a peach on each square then wrap the dough around them and pinch the edges to seal them and make the dumplings.
8. Place a large salted pot of water over high heat. Bring it to a boil.
9. Drop it in 4 to 5 dumplings. Bring them to a rolling boil for 22 min while stirring them every 11 min.
10. Drain the dumplings and place them aside. Repeat the process with the remaining dumplings.
11. Place a small pan over medium heat. Heat in it the brown sugar with butter to make the sauce.
12. Drizzle the butter sauce over the dumplings. Serve them with some ice cream.
13. Enjoy.

Sharp Cheesy Potato Casserole

Prep Time: 15 mins
Total Time: 45 mins

Servings per Recipe: 6
Calories 522.3
Fat 17.8g
Cholesterol 47.1mg
Sodium 831.1mg
Carbohydrates 70.1g
Protein 22.2g

Ingredients

- 2 tbsp extra virgin olive oil
- 6 large potatoes, boiled and cubed
- 2 C. cottage cheese
- 1 C. sour cream
- 1 tsp salt
- 1 onion, chopped
- 1 C. sharp cheddar cheese, grated
- 1/2 tsp Hungarian paprika

Directions

1. Before you do anything, preheat the oven to 350 F.
2. Stir the potatoes, cottage cheese, sour cream, salt and onions in a greased baking dish.
3. Top it with the grated cheese and paprika. Place the casserole in the oven and cook it for 32 min.
4. Serve your potato casserole warm.
5. Enjoy.

A VEGAN'S Potato Soup

⏺ Prep Time: 30 mins
🕐 Total Time: 50 mins

Servings per Recipe: 6
Calories   161 kcal
Fat   3.1 g
Carbohydrates   31.3g
Protein   3.8 g
Cholesterol   1 mg
Sodium   1196 mg

Ingredients

4 large carrots, thinly sliced
2 large potatoes, thinly sliced
1 large onion, thinly sliced
1/4 medium head green cabbage, thinly sliced
2 cloves garlic, smashed
6 C. chicken stock
1 tbsp olive oil

1/4 tsp dried thyme
1/4 tsp dried basil
1 tsp dried parsley
1 tsp salt
ground black pepper to taste

Directions

1. In a large soup pan, mix together the carrots, potatoes, onion, cabbage, garlic, chicken broth, olive oil, thyme, basil, parsley, salt and pepper on medium-high heat and bring to a boil.
2. Cook for about 20 minutes.
3. Remove from the heat and keep aside to cool slightly.
4. In a blender, add the soup in batches and pulse till smooth.

Beef Based Corn Potato Soup

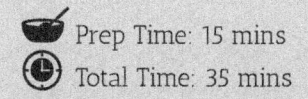

Prep Time: 15 mins
Total Time: 35 mins

Servings per Recipe: 8
Calories   156 kcal
Fat   3.7 g
Carbohydrates   29 g
Protein   4.1 g
Cholesterol   8 mg
Sodium   848 mg

Ingredients

4 potatoes, peeled and quartered
1 (14 oz.) can whole kernel corn
1/2 C. chopped onion
2 tbsp butter
1 tbsp beef base
1 tsp salt
1/4 tsp red pepper flakes
1/8 tsp ground black pepper
water, as needed

Directions

1. In a large pan, mix together the potatoes, corn, onion, butter, beef base, salt, red pepper flakes, black pepper and enough water over the mixture to cover by 2 inches and bring to a boil.
2. Reduce the heat to medium-low and simmer for about 20 minutes.
3. Remove from the heat and keep aside to cool slightly.
4. In a blender, add the soup in batches and pulse till smooth.

VEGETABLE SOUP from Bogota

Prep Time: 45 mins
Total Time: 1 hr 55 mins

Servings per Recipe: 6
Calories 488.5
Fat 13.1g
Cholesterol 96.7mg
Sodium 963.4mg
Carbohydrates 54.2g
Protein 42.9g

Ingredients

2 tbsp olive oil
1/2 C. coarsely chopped onion
2 medium tomatoes, peeled, seeded and coarsely chopped
2 lb. boneless stewing beef, cut into 1 1/2-inch cubes
1 large bay leaf
1 tsp ground cumin
1/2 tsp dried oregano
1/4 tsp turmeric
1/2 tsp finely chopped garlic
2 tsp salt
6 whole black peppercorns
3 C. cold water
2 tsp cider vinegar
3 medium potatoes, peeled and cut lengthwise into 1/4-inch slices and then into 1/2-inch wide strips
4 medium carrots, cut 1/4-inch x 1/2-inch strips
4 trimmed celery ribs, washed and cut into 2-inch lengths
1 lb fresh green peas, shelled
4 ears corn, shucked and cut into 2-inch lengths

Directions

1. In a heavy 3-4-qt. flameproof casserole, heat the oil on medium heat and tilt the casserole to coat the bottom evenly.
2. Add the onions and cook and sauté for about 4-5 minutes.
3. Stir in the tomatoes and cook for about 3 minutes.
4. Add the beef, bay leaf, cumin, oregano, turmeric, garlic, salt, peppercorns, water and vinegar and stir to combine.
5. Reduce the heat to very low and simmer, covered for about 30 minutes.
6. Stir in the potatoes, carrots and celery and simmer, covered for about 20 minutes.
7. Stir in the peas and corn and simmer, covered for about 10 minutes.
8. Serve hot.

ENJOY THE RECIPES?

KEEP ON COOKING WITH 6 MORE FREE COOKBOOKS!

Visit our website and simply enter your email address to join the club and receive your 6 cookbooks.

http://booksumo.com/magnet

https://www.instagram.com/booksumopress/

https://www.facebook.com/booksumo/

Printed in Great Britain
by Amazon